color

the quilter's guide

CHRISTINE
BARNES

Credits

Editor-in-Chief .... Kerry I. Smith

Technical Editor .... Ursula Reikes

Managing Editor .... Judy Petry

Copy Editor .... Tina Cook

Proofreader .... Melissa Riesland

Design Director .... Cheryl Stevenson

Text and Cover Designer .... Sandy Wing

Design Assistant .... Claudia L'Heureux

Illustrator .... Laurel Strand

Illustration Assistant .... Robin Strobel

Photographer .... Brent Kane

Additional Photo Credits

"Brown Quilt," pg. 14 .... Jon Jensen

"Under the Knife," pg. 22 .... Roger Schreiber

"The River of Dreams," pg. 51 .... Steve Buckley

"When You Are Very Still," pg. 54
"Ordinary Joy," pg. 55
"The Greenhouse Effect," pg. 82 .... Bill Bachhuber

"Baltimore Memories," pg. 61 .... Sharon Reisdorph

"Freehand 6: Settling In," pg. 70
.... Hester + Hardaway, Photographers

"Alpenglow," pg. 71 .... Kristi Kelly, Amaranth Studios

"Royal Palms of Paia," pg. 72
"Persephone's Plight," pg. 75
.... Norton Photography of Cincinnati

"Kaleidoscopic XIII: Random Acts of Color," pg. 77
.... Karen Bell

"Fourpatch I: June Backyard," pg. 80
"Hair Raising," pg. 82 .... Neal Farris

Title page quilt:

Sidestreet I by Melody Johnson, 1995, Cary, Illinois, 35" x 25". An electric combination of blue-greens and oranges illustrates the color phenomenon known as simultaneous contrast. Where intense complements abut, the eye sees a fine, dark line, which Melody describes as a "dancing edge."

Color: The Quilter's Guide

©1997 by Christine Barnes

That Patchwork Place, Inc.

PO Box 118

Bothell, WA 98041-0118 USA

Printed in Hong Kong

02 01 00 99 98 97 6 5 4 3 2 1

**Library of Congress
Cataloging-in-Publication Data**

Barnes, Christine.
    Color : the quilter's guide / Christine Barnes.
        p.   cm.
    ISBN 1-56477-164-4
    1. Patchwork quilts. 2. Color in textile crafts. I.
Title.
TT835.B267   1997
746.46—dc21   96-37060
                                                                    CIP

Dedication

To my uncle, David Barnes, for teaching me about color and encouraging me in every way.

Acknowledgments

So many talented people have had a hand in this book. Heartfelt thanks to the members of the Foothill Quilters' Guild and Pine Tree Quilt Guild who made many of the blocks and quilts you see throughout the book; to the talented designers who contributed quilts and instructions for the Color Studies chapter; and to the quilters whose work appears in the gallery and other chapters. Your love of color and dedication to your art inspire us all.

I greatly appreciated the opportunity to learn from two excellent teachers. Judi Warren opened my eyes to the creative possibilities of transparency. From Jean Ray Laury I gained valuable insight into color relationships.

It takes a great deal of fabric to put together a book about color. Many thanks to FASCO/Fabric Sales Company, Inc., Hoffman of California, Mission Valley Textiles, Inc., RJR Fashion Fabrics, Cherrywood Fabrics, Inc., and P & B Textiles for furnishing their beautiful fabrics.

A special thank-you to John Palmer of Autometrix for the precision cutting of the color-block pieces and the color wheels.

Finally, to my mother, Marjorie Barnes, and my dear friends Hawton-Hill and Heidi Emmett, thanks for the encouragement.

contents

a sense of color

Sitting in my sewing room amid a clutter of color, choosing fabrics for one more sample block, I wonder how to sum up my thoughts. For more than a year, color has captivated me, beckoned me, and cheered me. I've often thought that there could be no better project than writing a book about color. Lucky me!

Insight into color, however, has not always come easily. As soon as I answered one color question, a new, more difficult one would find a voice, teasing and challenging me to explain what seemed inexplicable. Why does goldenrod bring a group of fabrics to life, while buttercup looks all wrong? Can quilters learn to love the color wheel? Does anyone really care about simultaneous contrast? And most important, How do I address the real concerns quilters have about color?

In trying to answer these questions, I learned valuable color lessons, and the pleasures far outweighed the frustrations. My hope is that the book you now hold in your hands will answer many of your color questions and inspire you to see and work with color in new ways.

You might start by putting color theory in its proper place. Studying color is not an end in itself; it is simply the means to making better quilts. Once grounded in the fundamentals, you are free to discard stale color schemes, free to flirt with dangerous colors—in short, free to be brave with color. On the practical side, color knowledge cuts down on unnecessary experimentation and gives you a head start when you begin to design a quilt.

To use color effectively, you need a good grasp of the basics. Promise yourself that you will learn, and not just read about, the color terms and concepts in this book. Read

told by others to trust your intuition, but, as far as you can tell, you have none. Even more confusing, you hear that color is subjective (true) and that there are no rules (not true). These generalizations may discourage you and convince you that a feel for color is something you don't have and can't acquire.

I'm happy to tell you that you are absolutely wrong. After reading color books, visiting quilt shows, and studying hundreds of slides and photos, I have come to a simple but encouraging conclusion about color and talent: Intuition is experience. That's right: Intuition is experience. What you take for raw talent in a quilter is partly the result of hard work and experience; you just haven't seen his or her early quilts to appreciate the progress. When an outstanding quilter says, "I work intuitively," pay more attention to the "work" part of that sentence and less to the notion of intuition. Through hard work you gain experience, which blossoms into intuition, also known as good color sense.

You might also like to know that accomplished quilters know about color— they know what causes intense colors to vibrate when placed side by side, which colors make up a triadic combination, and how to achieve luminosity with fabrics. They aren't working blind; they consciously apply the elements and principles of color to their quilts.

Which leads me to a final cheerful conclusion: You, too, can do color. Did you hear me? You can do color! Fabric is not free, but the magic of color is, and any color combination is yours for the asking. Who can resist the lure?

the text, study the examples, and then read the text again if necessary. Understanding the difference between value and intensity is especially important because these two characteristics, as much as color, determine the visual impact of a quilt.

Color concepts are a staple of classic color theory, but the real magic comes from the relationships between colors. It is, after all, the juxtaposition and interaction of colors that make a quilt sing. To learn the most about color relationships, study the color wheels on pages 10–11 and refer to them often as you read the text and photo captions. Your efforts to observe and understand color will be well rewarded. When you shop for fabric, you will feel comfortable including colors you thought were beyond your palette. And one day, while browsing the bolts, you will see a sophisticated fabric and say to yourself, "Look at that—analogous yellows, oranges, and reds cooled by complementary blues. Nice!"

At this point, you may be thinking that understanding color concepts and relationships isn't going to do you any good because you have no color sense. You are

the language of color

Learning the language of color is a little like studying a foreign language before going on vacation: the more fluent you are, the more fun you'll have. If you're put off by the thought of a long list of definitions, relax. This chapter uses easy-to-understand terms and lots of examples to bring color concepts to life.

Hue

Hue is just another word for color. Sky blue and crimson are hues, as are softer colors such as celadon and lavender. This book uses the terms hue and color interchangeably. Turn to the color wheels on pages 10–11 to see the twelve pure hues.

Value

Color comes first in the minds of most quilters, but the study of color really begins with value. If you've ever made a quilt that disappointed you, chances are the problem was related to value, not color. Experienced quilters often say that you can use any colors, as long as the values are right.

Light, medium, and dark values are also known as tints, tones, and shades.

The term *value* refers to the lightness or darkness of a color. Tints are light-value versions of pure hues. Peach is a tint of orange, iris is a tint of blue-violet, pistachio is a tint of green.

One common misconception is that tints are always pastels. Not true. Any color that is lighter than the full-strength color is a tint. Melon, coral, and azure are tints, but they are stronger than sweet, soft pastels. On the color wheels, tints lie just inside the hue rings. This book uses the terms *tint* and *light-value color* interchangeably.

Tones are medium-value colors such as terra-cotta (a tone of red-orange) and mauve (a tone of red-violet). The word *tone* is often used to describe a color or group of colors, such as "blue tones." This book uses the term *medium-value color* to describe a tone.

Shades are dark-value versions of pure hues. Like tints, many shades have descriptive names—burnt sienna, midnight blue, and spice, to name a few. And like the term *tone*, *shade* is sometimes used to describe a particular color—"a shade of blue," for example. To avoid confusion, this book generally refers to shades as *dark-value colors*. On the color wheels, shades are in the outermost rings.

Keep in mind that every pure color has an intrinsic value, and it varies around the color wheel. Yellow, the hue closest to white in terms of lightness, is the lightest-value color; violet, the hue closest to black, is the darkest-value color. Blue-green and red-orange are medium-value colors.

Value creates depth. Contrasts in value create a sense of depth in a quilt because we perceive different values as being on different planes. Tumbling Blocks and Attic Windows are among the best-known traditional blocks that suggest depth through value.

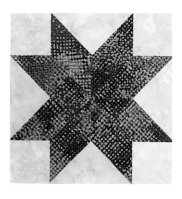

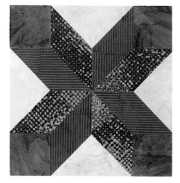

Value determines the design and establishes depth. The placement of light, medium, and dark values turns a two-dimensional Eight Pointed Star into a three-dimensional one.

The greater the value contrast, the greater the sense of depth. Yellow shapes appear to merge with a white background because yellow is close to white in value. The same yellow shapes seem to come forward on a dark blue background because the values are far apart.

Value is relative. Seen individually, a fabric has a value that you can describe—it is either light, medium, or dark. But as soon as you put one fabric next to another, relative values shift, often dramatically. Against a dark background, a medium fabric appears light; against a light background, the same fabric looks dark.

This chameleon-like quality increases your design options. You might use the same medium-value fabric as a light piece among dark pieces in one block, and as a dark piece among light pieces in another.

Value determines the design. We say that we see in color, but in fact we see in value. More than color, the placement of light, medium, and dark values in a quilt determines the design. Log Cabin and Star blocks are popular designs that depend on

Value is relative: a medium-value color looks light or dark, depending on the value of the surrounding color.

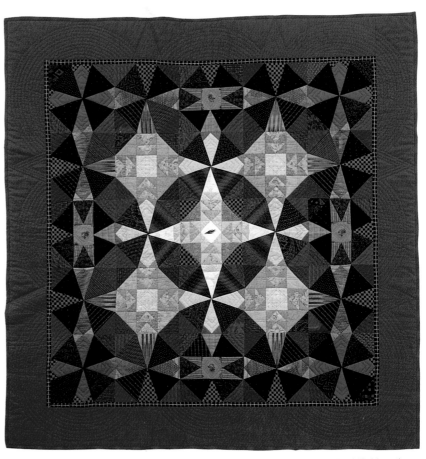

As the Crow Flies *by Susan M. Connoley, 1996, Gig Harbor, Washington, 62" x 62". More than color, value determines the design in this quilt, which is composed of Double Z, Capital T, and Kaleidoscope blocks. The colors are analogous, from orange through blue-violet.*

light-and-dark contrast. In quilts with gradated color, subtle shifts in value create smooth visual transitions.

Refer to page 84 in "A Color Workshop" for an exercise that demonstrates the role of value in determining a design and establishing depth.

Tip: Squinting lets you see value in spite of color. A reducing glass, the opposite of a magnifying glass, distances you from your design wall and makes value easier to discern. Many quilters view fabrics through a Ruby Beholder® or sheet of red cellophane to determine their value. A black-and-white photocopy will also tell you whether different values are holding their own or blending.

Winter Solstice *by Susan M. Connoley, 1996, 62" x 62". What a difference value makes! Using the same three blocks, Susan creates a dramatically different design. The colors are complementary red-orange and blue-green.*

Visual Temperature

The term *visual temperature* conjures up all sorts of mental images. Are colors really so hot that they have a fever, or so icy that they make you shiver? Not quite, but visual temperature is a key color characteristic, and you can use it to create powerful visual effects in your quilts.

If you draw an imaginary line on the color wheel from red-violet to yellow-green, all the colors to the left—yellows, oranges, and reds—are considered warm. In nature and the man-made world, warm colors are stimulating and energetic. Think of fiery geraniums at the height of summer, or the hot colors of advertising. In color theory, warm colors are often referred to as *advancing* colors because they seem nearer than they are.

Greens, blues, and violets are the cool hues; they're considered *receding* colors because they appear to be farther away. Cool colors are tranquil and soothing: visualize blue water, lush meadows, or hills covered with purple heather. In nature, the colors that you see in the distance are often cool.

Within color families, both warm and cool hues exist. Green, for example, is generally considered a cool color, but olive green (green with yellow) is visually warm, while sea green (green with blue) is cooler by comparison. In the red family, red-violet appears cooler than red-orange.

Even neutrals—black, white, gray, and very low-intensity hues—possess a visual temperature. Black is generally considered warm; white is cool. Some beiges have a pink or peach cast, while others are cool and steely. If you're having difficulty determining the visual temperature of neutral fabrics, look at them in a group.

Like value, visual temperature is relative. A warm color among cool colors will appear warm, but among even warmer colors it will look relatively cool. Red-violet against blue-green appears warm and seems to advance; the same red-violet against red-orange looks cool and appears to recede.

You can use your awareness of color temperature to enrich and balance a color scheme. A pale version of red-orange, a color that might be called "salmon blush," warms a cool scheme of blue and green tints. In the same way, blue cools down warm reds and oranges. Quilts that sparkle, old and new, almost always contain both warm and cool hues.

Refer to the exercise on page 85 in "A Color Workshop" to experiment with visual temperature.

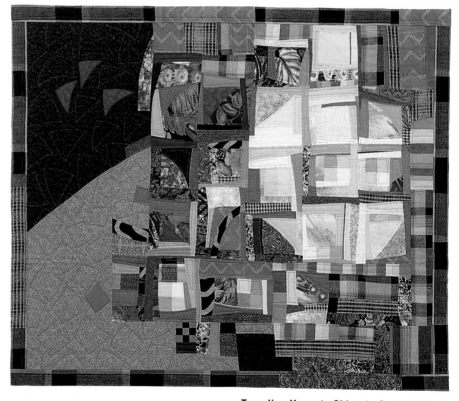

Traveling Years to Shine *by Susan Webb Lee, 1994, Weddington, North Carolina, 47" x 39". Warm and cool greens balance radiant reds, oranges, and yellows in this asymmetrical design. The composition, as much as the visual temperature, establishes a sense of space.*

It's easy to "take the temperature" of colors; most are decidedly warm or cool. Red-violet and yellow-green can be either, depending on surrounding colors.

Intensity

Intensity refers to the purity, or saturation, of a color. Even for beginning quilters, it's relatively easy to identify intense colors. These are the pure, poster-paint colors of childhood and the brilliant jewel tones of decorating and fashion. The hue rings of the color wheels (pages 10–11) contain the full-intensity colors.

If brilliant colors shout their color message, low-intensity colors speak in whispers. These are the quiet hues, colors such as sage, wheat, brick, and slate. The innermost rings of the color wheels feature light-value, low-intensity versions of the twelve hues, known as complement tints. (You'll learn more about these colors on page 12.)

Having just read about value, you may wonder, What's the difference between value and intensity? Value has to do with the lighter/darker aspect of color, while intensity has to do with its purer/duller quality. Low-intensity colors are not necessarily dark in value. Imagine a dull, dark navy blue and a light blue-gray. The navy blue is obviously a low-intensity, dark-value color. The light blue-gray, however, is low in intensity but light in value. To differentiate between value and intensity, it helps to think of each characteristic separately when you evaluate a color. Ask yourself, Is it light or dark? Then, Is it pure or dull?

Variations in intensity lend sophistication to a design and keep it from looking predictable. On the other hand, when you want to set a definite mood, strive to maintain some consistency in intensity. Folk colors, for example, tend to be low intensity, while contemporary colors are high intensity.

When you consider intensity in colors and fabrics, keep in mind the following:

- In general, intense colors advance, while low-intensity colors recede. However, if low-intensity shapes are large, they may advance; it all depends on the design. Value can also override intensity in

Intense colors are pure and brilliant; low-intensity colors are grayed and subdued.

determining which colors advance and which ones recede.

- The Law of Areas, a principle of classic color theory, suggests using intense colors in small areas of a design, as accents, and low-intensity colors in large areas.
- Colors placed on a black background appear more intense than the same colors on a white background.
- Intensity is relative: A color looks more intense when placed among duller colors; the same color looks less intense among purer colors.

Refer to the exercise on page 86 in "A Color Workshop" to experiment with color intensity.

Town Planning 3 *by Michele Vernon, 1995, Falls Church, Virginia, 14" x 21". Low-intensity hues contrast with the more intense colors of the madras plaids. Black-and-white stripes, symbolic of city streets, unify the design.*

The Color Wheels

Yellow

Yellow-orange

Yellow-green

Shade

Hue

Green

Orange

Tint

Red-orange

Complement
tint

Blue-green

Red

Blue

Red-violet

Blue-violet

Violet

If you've never used a color wheel to make a quilt, you're not alone. Lots of quilters find the color wheel intimidating and confusing. The pure colors they see on a typical wheel—bright red, violet, and orange, for example—aren't the colors they use in their quilts. And the delicious colors they see at the quilt shop—sophisticated hues such as iris, cocoa, and cinnabar—can't be found on the standard color wheel. No wonder quilters ask, "Who needs a color wheel to make a quilt?"

You do! Becoming acquainted with the color wheel is well worth the time it takes. Within this circle are intriguing color

relationships and magical color cues that can turn so-so quilts into sensational ones. With knowledge and practice, you can learn to build a fresh color scheme or to fix one that doesn't quite work.

Using a color wheel is easier than you might expect. Begin by thinking of the intense colors in the hue ring as the *source* of the real-life colors you see in fabrics and quilts. Red-orange is the source of colors we call terra-cotta, salmon, and coral. Terra-cotta is a low-intensity, medium-value version of red-orange; salmon and coral are tints of red-orange. Intense red-orange may

be difficult to use in a quilt, but softer versions of this hue are easy on the eye.

Consider other pure colors: Green, violet, and orange may seem harsh together, too harsh for a quilt. Now imagine dark-value, low-intensity versions of these hues, colors you might call juniper, eggplant, and nutmeg. Don't they sound more inviting?

All colors, no matter how complex or subtle, come from the pure hues on the color wheel. Although the color wheel can't dictate colors for your quilts, it can help you visualize what will happen when colors are combined. And, if you have a color in mind for a quilt, the color wheel can help you

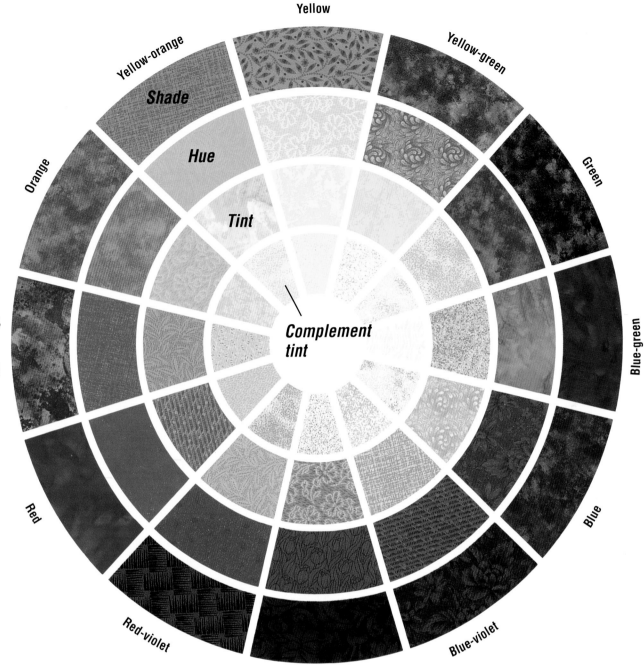

Yellow · Yellow-orange · Shade · Hue · Tint · Complement tint · Orange · Yellow-green · Green · Red-orange · Blue-green · Red · Blue · Red-violet · Blue-violet

build a variety of beautiful, balanced schemes.

To make the leap from color on the color wheel to color in your quilts, take the time to become familiar with the color wheels. Refer to them as you read about the different kinds of colors.

- Primary colors—red, blue, and yellow—combine to make all other colors. Full-strength primaries are difficult to use in large quantities. Low-intensity primaries—colors you might call brick, navy, and goldenrod—are less demanding; see page 87 for a combination of low-intensity primaries.

Violet

- Secondary colors lie midway between the primary colors on the color wheel. These colors are formed from the primaries:

    yellow + blue = green

    blue + red = violet

    red + yellow = orange

    Secondary colors are not as strong as primaries. In subdued versions, these hues abound in nature—think of green lichens, purple mountains, or orange streaks in river rock.

- Intermediate colors result from mixing a primary with an adjacent secondary

color. Blue (a primary) and green (a secondary) combine to make blue-green, an intermediate color. These colors are sometimes referred to as tertiaries.

- Neutrals set off and space out color, providing visual relief without altering the basic color relationships. Black, white, and gray are the true neutrals. Beiges are also considered neutrals, along with pale (light-value), dull (low-intensity) versions of other colors.

- Analogous colors lie next to each other on the color wheel. Green, blue-green, and blue are analogous; so are blue, blue-violet, violet, and red-violet.

- Complementary colors lie directly opposite each other on the color wheel. Red and green are complements, as are blue and orange, and yellow and violet. Intermediate colors, such as blue-green and red-orange, are complements too.

  Used in their full intensity, complements can be harsh. (The popular combination of Christmas red and green is an exception.) But as softer hues, they make up some of the most exquisite color combinations. You probably wouldn't choose intense violet and yellow for a quilt, but as tints that might be described as amethyst and butter cream, these complements are pleasing.

- Complement tints are less intense versions of tints. To understand this term, it helps to think about how an artist mixes paints. When an artist adds a small amount of one color to a large amount of its complement, a neutralized version of the main color results. The inner wedges on the color wheel show tints that contain a bit of the complement, colors known as complement tints. Light-value blue-violet with a small amount of yellow-orange, for example, neutralizes to a soft, sophisticated complement tint of lavender-blue. Pure red with a small amount of green neutralizes to a less-intense color that might be called brick.

The color wheels show only the complement tints, but this concept applies to medium-value colors (tones) and dark-value colors (shades) as well. In fact, many of the colors found in quilting fabrics are complement tones and shades.

"What Color Is That?"

Analyzing and identifying colors in fabrics can help you place them on the color wheel, the first step toward building or improving a color scheme. Some of the colors shown here are easily defined; others are complex, even ambiguous, versions of the pure hues on the color wheel. Before you read the captions, look at each fabric and try to tease apart its characteristics. What is the source color? The value? The visual temperature? The intensity? The more you look at color in fabric, the less you will wonder, "What color is that?"

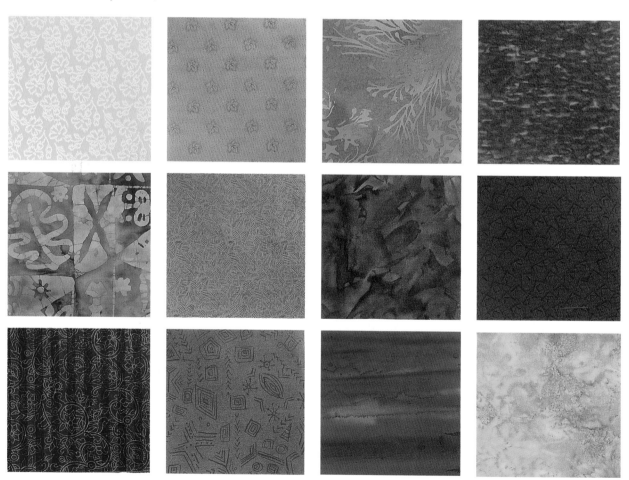

From top left: Lemon is a pure hue of yellow; chartreuse is a pure hue of yellow-green; emerald is a pure hue of green; peacock is a shade (dark value) of blue-green; sapphire is a tone (medium value) of blue; periwinkle is a tone of blue-violet; eggplant is a pure hue of violet; wild plum is a shade of red-violet; cranberry is a shade of red; cinnabar is a tone of red-orange; spice is a shade of orange; mango is a pure hue of yellow-orange.

color combinations

Something special happens when you combine colors in a quilt. Your least-favorite color sings in the company of its complement; unlikely colors turn into a beautiful blend of balanced hues; kindred colors look as though they were made for each other. In a sense, all colors go together if you know how to combine them. How colors interact in quilts is what this chapter is about.

On the next eight pages, you'll find discussions and examples of ten classic color combinations. You'll notice that some of the blocks and quilts are loose—to put it mildly—interpretations of the combinations. These examples illustrate one of the most important lessons you can learn about color combinations: there are no color formulas! You are free to wander around the color wheel and include colors that lie beyond the structure of the classic combination. You are just as free to choose slightly different versions of the colors—a yellow that is more orange than yellow, for example, or a green that is nearly blue. The classic combinations are just a place to begin a quilt design.

As you look at these blocks and quilts, keep in mind that a great color scheme doesn't just happen. It takes experimentation and a willingness to keep trying until you find a winning combination. Better to invest the time you need to develop your color plan fully than to later wish that you had used a different red. Your quilt is worth the effort.

Neutral

When your goal is an understated color scheme, consider a neutral combination. Because color is minimal in neutral schemes, their success depends on strong light/dark contrast and pattern variety. Vary the values throughout the design, and be sure to use a mix of pattern scales and styles (pages 26–27). Low-intensity colors,

such as brick, indigo, and olive, brighten neutrals without overpowering them.

Exquisite neutral combinations exist in the natural world—objects such as rock, bark, and driftwood display a surprising array of neutral hues. Neutrals also serve as quiet backdrops for intense natural color. Think of brilliant pink or yellow blossoms on low-intensity, gray-green cacti, or one just-fallen leaf, still vibrant, lying among faded leaves.

Chain *by Gigi Phillips, 1996, Penn Valley, California. In a neutral color combination, black, white, and gray function as light, medium, and dark values. Neutral schemes rely on variations in pattern and texture for their success.*

Winter Aspens *by Elizabeth A. Lonnquist, 1995, Citrus Heights, California, 44" x 59". A neutral palette allowed Elizabeth to fully explore value and visual temperature without the distractions of color or intensity. A black-and-white photo by Ansel Adams inspired her design.*

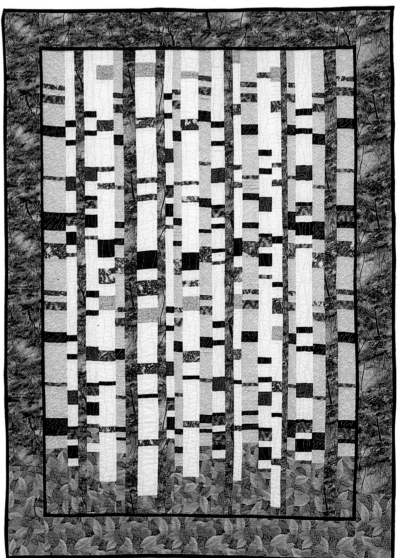

Monochromatic

Quilters often think that monochromatic ("one color") combinations are automatically dull, but they don't have to be. Some of the most sophisticated schemes consist of colors from the same color family. The key to success in a monochromatic scheme is variety in value, temperature, intensity, pattern, and texture. Put another way, a monochromatic scheme relies on contrasts other than color. A block that calls for more, rather than fewer, fabrics will give you the most options for creating contrast in a one-color quilt.

Monochromatic schemes are conceptually simple, yet they can be surprisingly difficult to achieve. When a monochromatic scheme doesn't work, the problem often lies with value. Without a sweep of values, from light to medium to dark, a one-color quilt can look flat. Try for enough contrast in value to differentiate the block pieces, but not so much that the pieces pull away from each other. Or, you may want to do just the opposite, blurring the lines between pieces by juxtaposing closely related values.

Slight variations in visual temperature are "allowed" in a monochromatic scheme. As you learned on page 8, there are warm and cool versions of every color. In a quilt with green pieces on a white background, you might include slightly warmer greens that approach yellow-green, and slightly cooler greens that tend toward blue-green. If you want to maintain the one-color harmony, however, don't get carried away with varying the visual temperature. When you go too far in either direction on the color wheel, a monochromatic scheme becomes an analogous one.

Variations in intensity add depth and sophistication to a monochromatic scheme. In an all-blue quilt, one blue might be clear and pure, while another is slightly grayed. Make the differences subtle or great, depending on the effect you're after.

In a monochromatic scheme, especially when your color range is very narrow,

variety in pattern scale and pattern style (pages 26–27) is essential. Monochromatic color combinations also benefit from doses of neutral color. Patterned neutrals, particularly black-and-white stripes, dots, and geometrics, separate the color and give the eye a place to rest.

Dahlias *by Laura Munson Reinstatler, 1996, Mill Creek, Washington. A monochromatic combination allows for slightly different versions of the same hue. Light values space out the intense color; red-violet extends the scheme.*

Brown Quilt *by Maggie Potter, 1994, Walnut Creek, California, 61" x 68". Low-intensity colors combine for a monochromatic effect in Maggie's interpretation of Old Tippecanoe. The prints vary from block to block, but the relative values stay the same. The intricate one-color border lets the focus fall on the blocks.*

Analogous

If you start with a monochromatic scheme and move in either direction or both directions on the color wheel to include adjacent colors, you'll have an analogous scheme. To be a true analogous combination, all of the colors must share a common color. In a combination of yellow-orange, yellow, and yellow-green, for example, yellow is the common color.

The obvious question is, How many colors make up an analogous color combination? There are several answers, all of them correct. Any three adjacent colors on the color wheel constitute an analogous combination. Expanding the scheme, an analogous combination can consist of the colors that lie between two primaries and include one of those primaries. For example, the colors between the primaries blue and red are blue-violet, violet, and red-violet. Add blue or red to these three hues, and you have a four-color analogous scheme. Remember, the key is a color common to all of the colors in the group. In an analogous combination of blue, blue-violet, violet, and red-violet, blue is the common color.

A more expansive analogous scheme takes in all of the colors that share the same primary, not counting the direct complements. Sound complicated? It's not. From red-orange around the wheel clockwise to blue-green, all the colors contain primary yellow. The colors vary in the degree of yellow, but they all have some. Drop the complements red-orange and blue-green, and you're left with a far-ranging, distantly related group of five colors.

As in neutral and monochromatic color schemes, analogous combinations rely heavily on a mix of values (light to dark) and intensities (bright and dull). In a broad analogous scheme, visual temperature comes into play too. An analogous combination that extends from red-violet through blue-green, for example, is more balanced in visual temperature than a narrow scheme of yellow-orange, orange, and red-orange.

To keep an analogous scheme from looking too predictable, vary the quantities of the colors and make one color an intense accent. The pure color will advance and seem brighter, whether it's warm or cool. This strategy is particularly effective when the other colors are low in intensity. In a combination of low-intensity red, red-violet, violet, and blue-violet, for example, an accent of intense periwinkle (blue-violet) becomes a jewel of color among the duller hues.

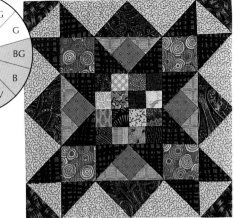

Best of All by Carol Walsh, 1996, Meadow Vista, California. This cool analogous scheme stretches from blue-green through violet. Carol achieves the illusion of luminosity (page 22) by the careful placement of light brights and dull darks.

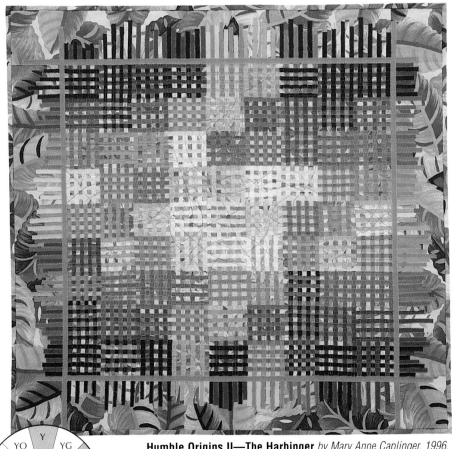

Humble Origins II—The Harbinger by Mary Anne Caplinger, 1996, Moravian Falls, North Carolina, 51" x 48". Analogous hues lighten as they move from the edge inward; soft yellow provides a warm accent. The quilt is composed of raw-edge strips that are woven and machine quilted.

Direct Complement

If monochromatic and analogous combinations are the quiet ones in the color crowd, complementary schemes are definitely the extroverts. Because they lie opposite each other on the color wheel, complements are automatically balanced in terms of visual temperature: Blue cools down orange; yellow warms up violet; green tempers red.

The history of complements helps to explain their natural balance and visual energy. M.E. Chevreul, a 17th-century French scientist interested in art, discovered that if you stare at a field of red for a minute or so, then look at a white sheet of paper, you will see an afterimage of green. The nerves in the retina, exhausted from staring at the red, "see" green in an attempt to balance vision. The word *complement* means "to complete." In other words, to your eye, the color green completes the color red, and vice versa.

The classic ratios for full-intensity complements of primary and secondary colors are ¼ yellow to ¾ violet; ⅔ blue to ⅓ orange; and ½ red to ½ green. You're not required to follow these ratios of course, but with the exception of red and green, a scheme is generally more pleasing when used in unequal quantities, with the cooler complement dominating. One way to include an accent of the warmer complement is to use a fabric that contains small quantities of the color.

Complements that consist of primary and secondary colors tend to be harsher than intermediate complements. Blue and orange (a primary and secondary), for example, are stronger than blue-green and red-orange (intermediates). The presence of two colors in an intermediate color softens the contrast.

All complements are easier to live with when the colors are less intense. Full-strength red and green are visually demanding; "trellis green" and "peony pink" are gentle by comparison.

Feel free to expand a complementary scheme to include other colors. To a yellow and violet combination, you might add green for a softer, more natural look. To orange and blue, introduce accents of red-violet and yellow-green. Remember, the classic color combinations are a place to begin a color scheme.

Freesias *by Laura Munson Reinstatler, 1996, Mill Creek, Washington. A combination of yellow and violet illustrates the classic color concept of using complements in unequal quantities.*

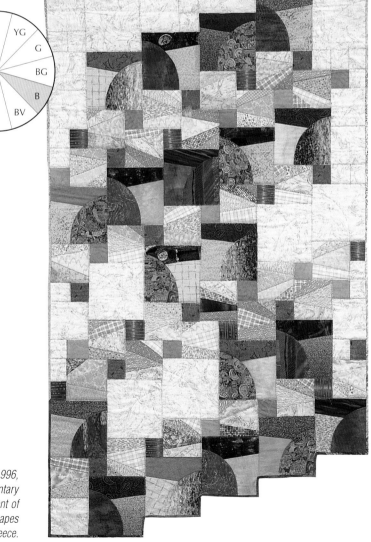

If White Is Air, What Is Orange? *by Kerry I. Smith, 1996, Bainbridge Island, Washington, 43¼" x 71¼". Complementary orange and blue resonate in this tessellated design, reminiscent of intricate tiling patterns. Kerry was inspired by architectural shapes silhouetted against the sea in Greece.*

Split Complement

A split complement is one of the easiest and most versatile color combinations for quilters. This three-color scheme consists of one color and the colors that lie on each side of its complement. In other words, you split the complement into the two adjacent colors. More subtle than a direct complement, a split complement has the harmony of related colors, with the pizzazz of a complement.

Refer to the color wheels on pages 10–11 as you read about the structure of the following split complement: Start with yellow, a primary. Yellow's complement is violet, a secondary. If you split violet into red-violet and blue-violet, you create a split complement of yellow, red-violet, and blue-violet. If this combination sounds harsh, visualize a quilt in lighter, less intense versions of these hues—butter cream (a tint of yellow), fuchsia (a hue of red-violet), and iris (a tint of blue-violet).

You can also begin a split complement with an intermediate color, such as red-orange. Its complement is blue-green, and the colors adjacent to blue-green are, of course, blue and green. Again, if these colors sound too strong in their pure form, imagine them as medium-value, low-intensity hues—earth red, Southampton blue, and awning green. To any split complement, you are free to add accents of other colors, such as a dash of goldenrod (a dark-value yellow) to the combination just described.

Theoretically, you can't begin a split complement with a secondary color because its opposite, a primary, is not made up of adjacent colors; that is, a primary can't be split. But in practice, the colors on each side of a primary harmonize with the primary's complement. Although orange, blue-green, and blue-violet are not a true split complement, they are still pleasing to the eye, especially as softer hues.

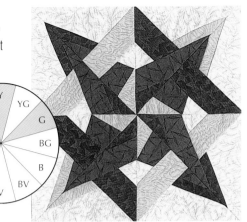

Manhattan by Sandra Bruce, 1996, Nevada City, California. A split complement of red-violet, yellow, and green is a fitting scheme for a complex block. Near-solids and subtle textures are good choices for a design with small pieces.

Double Complement

Two adjacent colors on the color wheel and their direct complements make up a double complementary combination. Yellow-orange and blue-violet, and orange and blue are double complements. This combination is really a hybrid of analogous and complementary combinations; the complements provide the contrast, while the adjacent colors contribute harmony to the scheme.

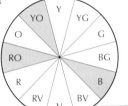

Reveille by Elaine Plogman, 1996, Cincinnati, Ohio, 36" x 36". In this split complement of blue, yellow-orange, and red-orange, the warm oranges advance while the cool blues recede. Accent colors soften the scheme.

Double Split Complement

Once you understand the structure of a split complement, you'll find it easy to develop a double split complement. This combination offers more variety than a split complement, yet it is still beautifully balanced. It can also be a bit of a challenge if you choose to work with intense colors.

To construct this color combination, begin with a pair of complements, such as intermediate red-violet and yellow-green. Split each of the colors into the adjacent colors: red-violet into red and violet, yellow-green into yellow and green. If these hues seem strident, imagine less intense versions, colors you might call crab apple (red), plum (violet), straw (yellow), and pistachio (green). Or consider the four colors as true pastels: blush (a tint of red), lilac (a tint of violet), cream (a tint of yellow), and mint (a tint of green).

As in a split complement, it is technically impossible to split a primary color because the primaries aren't made up of other colors, but in practice, a double split complement that starts with a primary and a secondary color will be pleasing because the colors are related and balanced.

It's essential to include a variety of values in a double split complement. Also vary the intensities of the colors to prevent unwanted simultaneous contrast (page 24). Accents of unrelated colors can add interest to the scheme and keep it from looking like a color formula.

You'll have the most success with a double split complement if you use the four colors in different quantities. Again, the Law of Areas suggests that you use the lighter, less intense colors for the large areas and the darker, more intense colors for the small areas. In a quilt based on the double split complement described above, you might use straw for the background, pistachio and crab apple for the main pieces, and plum as the accent.

If a quilt design calls for equal quantities of the four colors, it's important to use a variety of values, intensities, patterns, and textures; otherwise, the colors will fight for your attention. It also helps to include as many different versions of each color as you can find—a red-violet that is a little more red than violet, for example, and a yellow-green that is closer to yellow than to green.

Mollie's Choice by Patrice Sims, 1996, Loomis, California. A scheme loosely based on a double split complement of blue and orange, and red and green balances warm and cool hues. Yellow-green extends the combination.

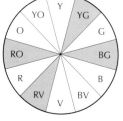

Free As a Bird by Wendy Hill, 1996, Sunriver, Oregon, 73" x 73". A double split complement of blue-green and red-orange, and yellow-green and red-violet pulsates in this spirited interpretation of Wild Goose Chase. Wendy deliberately used equal quantities of the colors to create a pleasing visual tension.

Triad

Triads are among the most harmonious and most favored of all color combinations. A triad consists of three colors that are equidistant on the color wheel; if you connect the colors with imaginary lines, an equilateral triangle forms. Another easy way to find a triad is to choose every fourth color on the color wheel.

There are four possible triadic color combinations:

- Red, yellow, and blue. A trio of primaries is the strongest of the triads. You often find green, a secondary color, included in a combination of primaries; green exerts a cooling, calming effect on the yellow and red.
- Green, violet, and orange. A triad of secondary colors is more complex and subtle than a triad of primaries. Dark-value, low-intensity secondaries are intriguing; see "Stars Out of Africa" on page 111. Lighter, brighter versions of these three colors are lively in combination; see "Tipsy Tiles" on page 118. Light-value secondaries are colors that might be described as lichen (a tint of green), orchid (a tint of violet), and apricot (a tint of orange).
- Red-violet, blue-green, and yellow-orange (see photo on page 33), or red-orange, yellow-green, and blue-violet (see photos on pages 92–93). Triads of intermediate colors are often visually softer than the primary or secondary combinations.

To prevent visual tension in a triadic scheme, make one of the colors dominant and let the other two play subordinate roles. It also helps to vary the values and intensities throughout the quilt.

Tetrad

Four colors equidistant on the color wheel make up a tetradic combination. There are three possible tetrads:

- Red, green, blue-violet, and yellow-orange (see photo on page 89);
- Violet, yellow, blue-green, and red-orange (see photo on page 86);
- Blue, orange, red-violet, and yellow-green.

Because they come from all around the color wheel, the colors in a tetrad balance light and dark, warm and cool hues. Take a careful look at multi-colored quilting fabrics and you'll see a surprising number of tetradic color combinations. These fabrics make great lead fabrics (page 32) because they provide so many color cues. As in other multi-color combinations, it's best to vary the quantities, values, and intensities of the colors.

Harvest Basket by Tece Markel, 1996, Newcastle, California. A tetrad of red, green, blue-violet, and yellow-orange (extended to include violet and orange) is a fitting combination for this portrayal of summer's bounty.

Screen Saver by Myrna Raglin, 1996, Nevada City, California, 44" x 44". A near-triad of low-intensity blue-green, red-violet, and orange is in keeping with this sophisticated computer-inspired design. Yellow-orange is technically the correct third color in the triad, but orange exerts an equally powerful warming influence.

Polychromatic

Quilts of many colors fill quilt shows, magazines, and books, delighting quiltmakers and admirers alike. Why? Polychromatic quilts have a vitality and charm that monochromatic and analogous schemes sometimes lack. The popularity of scrappy quilts and gloriously colored art quilts proves that when it comes to color, many quilters clearly think more is better.

If you're planning to make a polychromatic quilt, review the color characteristics of hue, value, visual temperature, and intensity (pages 6–9). Because a polychromatic scheme includes many different colors, perhaps every color on the color wheel, you will achieve balance between warm and cool colors without trying. That's part of the appeal of polychromatic quilts: they satisfy our desire for color balance.

If color and visual temperature vary more or less beyond your control, how do you unify a polychromatic quilt? The key is to maintain some consistency in the other two color characteristics, value and intensity.

Value is a powerful unifying factor. The colors may vary, but when the relative values repeat from block to block (page 34), a polychromatic quilt looks unified. Don't confuse the repetition of relative values with using fabrics of only one value. A polychromatic quilt with light, medium, and dark values in the same positions in each block will be both varied and unified. A quilt with only light-value or dark-value fabrics will probably look flat and monotonous.

Disparate colors that are similar in intensity can also unify a polychromatic quilt. Similar doesn't mean identical, however; be sure to vary the intensities slightly, or the quilt will look dull.

Neutrals play an important role in polychromatic quilts. Try bridging the visual gap between fabrics that look wrong by placing a neutral fabric between them. Traditionally, neutral or same-color sashing unifies multi-colored blocks. In contemporary quilts, neutrals provide visual relief

from colors that might otherwise compete.

Don't underestimate the importance of pattern and texture in polychromatic quilts. You will achieve variety in pattern style and texture; it just happens when you combine lots of different fabrics. To avoid chaos, repeat one or more pattern styles, such as florals, stripes, and plaids.

See page 88 in "A Color Workshop" for an exercise in classic color combinations.

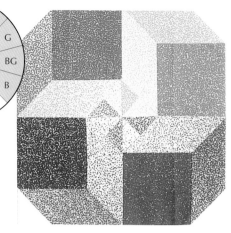

Pinwheel Block *by Richele Christensen, 1996, Citrus Heights, California. Light, medium, and dark values from a polychromatic palette tease the imagination into seeing three-dimensional forms.*

Ocean Waves *by Carolyn Miller, 1994, Santa Cruz, California, 80" x 95". In Carolyn's polychromatic rendition of this traditional favorite, low-intensity hues unify the design. Contrasting values keep the eye moving and make the quiet colors dance.*

Color Combinations in Fabrics

You'll find exciting examples of classic color combinations in many multi-colored fabrics. Textile designers are, after all, professional colorists, and you can learn from their creativity and expertise. This page shows nine examples of color combinations in fabrics. Analyze each combination, referring to the thumbnail color wheel to see the color relationships. Then analyze the value and intensity of the colors. Although most multi-colored fabrics contain a range of values, intensity is usually consistent.

Near-triad of red-violet, blue-green, and yellow

Triad of red, blue, and yellow

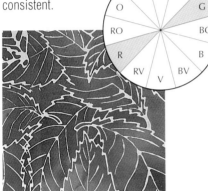

Direct complement of low-intensity red and green

Analogous yellow-orange, orange, red-orange, and red

Tetrad of red, green, yellow-orange, and blue-violet

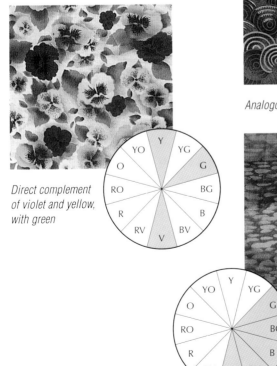

Direct complement of violet and yellow, with green

Analogous blue, violet, and red-violet

Split complement of yellow, red-violet, and blue-violet, with green

Analogous green, blue-green, blue, blue-violet, and violet

special effects

Special effects are the quilter's magic tricks. When these illusions work, colors interact and appear to glow, mix, vibrate, and retreat before our eyes, leaving us to wonder who is in control. Color has the power to deceive, and we are pleased to be fooled! Following are discussions of four intriguing color effects and ways to achieve them in quilts.

Luminosity

A quilt glows when radiant light appears to come from within the quilt or behind its surface. You can create this special effect by manipulating color, value, and intensity. Here's how:

To be convincing, the color that glows must be lighter in value than the surrounding colors. Hues that are naturally light in value, such as yellow and orange, glow more readily than violet and blue, which are

Under the Knife by Janet Steadman, 1995, Clinton, Washington, 43" x 34". The juxtaposition of light and dark values contributes to the sense of luminosity in this improvisational quilt. Slivers of intense, light-value colors appear to glow in the company of duller, darker colors.

naturally dark in value. The value contrast between the glow and the surrounding area can be subtle and still be effective, as long as the difference is discernible. With colors that are similar in value, the illusion is more of a shimmer than a glow.

Intense, pure color glows more when placed against a low-intensity background. This relationship is relative—a slightly dulled yellow still glows against a backdrop

of violet that is even duller. High-intensity hand-dyed fabrics, especially those that look dappled or mottled, are radiant against dark, smoldering backgrounds.

Area also plays a role in luminosity. In general, the most effective glow occurs when a small area of light, pure color is surrounded by a relatively large area of dark, dull color. This rule is meant to be broken, however, and you can achieve luminosity over a large area as long as the glowing color is surrounded by darker, less intense color at the edges.

Luminosity is equally impressive in traditional and contemporary quilts. Quiltmakers from the past, in particular the Amish, achieved stunning luminosity effects using basic shapes and intense colors, often in combination with black. Contemporary quilt designers create equally dazzling examples of luminosity using both traditional and innovative shapes: see "Fourpatch I: June Backyard" (page 80), "AutoFiction: Building Blocks" (page 77), and "The Aurora" (page 76).

See page 90 in "A Color Workshop" for an exercise in luminosity.

Stars and Crosses *by Carol Walsh, 1993, Meadow Vista, California, 71" x 87". By placing the lighter values in the center and the slightly darker values near the edge, Carol creates a quilt washed in soft, expansive light. Fuchsia centers in the crosses turn a two-color quilt into a subtle split complement of green, red-orange, and red-violet.*

Transparency

Of all the special effects, transparency is the one guaranteed to please everyone. In a transparency, we see something that makes sense, even when we know it can't be true. Transparency illusions are easy to achieve once you understand the mechanics.

In this special effect, one transparent color appears to lie over another, and where the two colors overlap, a third logical color is formed. The original colors are the source colors; the color created is the mixed color.

A few tips will help you create successful transparency effects in your quilts:

- To fool the eye, the mixed color must be different enough from the source colors so that it reads as a distinct shape.
- The mixed color must be large enough to be noticed; a small shape will get lost among much larger shapes. A good rule of thumb is to make the mixed-color shape at least one-fifth the size of the combined source-color shapes.
- A transparency reads best when you can clearly see the source colors, as in the nine-patch crosses in "Back to Basics," above right.

You can achieve transparency through value, color, design, or a combination of these characteristics.

Value transparency. This, the simplest transparency, involves a light, medium, and dark value of one color; where the light and dark values overlap, a medium-value color is created. You can override logic and create a value transparency using unrelated colors as long as the values are distinctly different. In any value transparency, the source color closest in value to the mixed color will appear to be on top.

Dancing Shadows *by Gloria Hansen, 1995, Hightstown, New Jersey, 34" x 34". Offset piecing and shifting values suggest flickering light and transparent overlays in this animated quilt. Gloria designed the block by computer and hand painted or hand dyed all but two of the fabrics.*

Back to Basics *by Lynn J. Crook, 1994, Berkeley, California, 63" x 64". Simple color transparencies are most convincing when the ends of the source colors show and the mixed-color shapes are distinct. A masterful mix of neutral patterns and textures produces the soft-focus effect.*

Value-and-color transparency. Adding color to the equation strengthens the transparency effect. The mixed color should look like the logical combination of one source color that is light and a different source color that is dark. A light-value green and dark-value blue, for example, might overlap to create a medium-value blue-green.

Color-and-design transparency. In this transparency, the source colors appear in the mixed color, as if you had combined but not blended two colors. A color and design transparency requires a multi-colored mixed fabric and two fabrics that look like the logical sources of the multi-colored fabric. It's easiest to achieve this kind of transparency if you start with the mixed-color fabric and work backward to find fabrics in the source colors.

See page 91 in "A Color Workshop" for an exercise that explores transparency.

Simultaneous Contrast

The color interaction known as simultaneous contrast may sound complicated, but it's easy to understand once you see it in a block or quilt. Among the special effects, this one is perhaps the most dramatic. It's also the one that can occur when you least expect it—or want it.

Simultaneous contrast is related to the color phenomenon of successive contrast, also known as the afterimage effect. If you stare at a small square of pure red fabric for a minute or so and then look at a sheet of white paper, you will see a faint afterimage of green. That's because, after looking at red, your eye naturally sees green, the complement of red.

Now imagine what occurs when you place two complements, such as red and green, side by side in a quilt. You simultaneously see each color's complement, intensifying both colors and maximizing the contrast. Put another way, the red triggers an afterimage of green, intensifying the green, while the green triggers an afterimage of red, intensifying the red. Both colors appear brighter and purer. The effect is strongest at the edge where the two colors meet, which explains why complements placed side by side sometimes appear to vibrate. Like other special effects, simultaneous contrast also works with colors that aren't true complements, such as near-complementary green and orange.

Simultaneous contrast can also be subtle. Neutral gray next to violet appears yellowish because the eye tinges the gray with yellow, the complement of violet. The same gray looks bluish when placed next to orange because blue is the complement of orange.

Using the principle of simultaneous contrast, you can accentuate shapes by placing them next to complementary colors, or play down shapes by placing them next to analogous colors. Intense yellow-orange shapes on a backdrop of equally intense blue-violet will stand out,

while the same yellow-orange shapes on orange will blend with the background.

If simultaneous contrast causes unwanted visual tension, you can reduce the effect by varying the values. Once a light/dark contrast exists, simultaneous contrast diminishes. The same is true of intensity: lowering the intensity of one or both of the complements cancels the effect of simultaneous contrast.

See page 90 in "A Color Workshop" for an exercise in simultaneous contrast.

Refraction *by Libby Lehman, 1994, Dallas, Texas, 55½" x 40". Simultaneous contrast is greatest when the adjacent colors are pure and complementary, or approximately complementary, such as the blue and blue-green bars and the orange background in the middle scale. Where the colors are similar, the effect is lessened.*

Geranium *by Velda Newman, 1993, Nevada City, California, 82" x 98". (From the collection of John M. Walsh III.) In this stunning quilt, full-intensity colors vibrate in each other's company. The simultaneous contrast is just as strong with red and blue as it is with complementary red and green.*

Depth

You can boil down the strategies for creating depth in a quilt to one word: contrast. When fabrics similar in color, value, visual temperature, or intensity are placed side by side, they appear to merge. Contrast, however, fools the eye and produces the illusion of depth on a two-dimensional surface. Here's a quick review of the variables that can create the illusion of depth in a design.

Value determines depth. There is no rule that says light values always advance and dark values always recede, or the other way around. Depth depends as much on composition as on value. However, the stronger the contrast between light and dark values, the greater the illusion of depth. Yellow advances when placed next to black because yellow is naturally light in value, and black couldn't be darker. Violet next to the same black will lurk in the background because both are dark-value colors.

Visual temperature influences depth. In general, warm colors advance and cool colors recede. Value, however, often overrides visual temperature: dark green (a cool color) may advance while pale peach (a warm color) recedes.

Intensity affects depth. Pure, intense colors tend to come forward, while low-intensity colors keep their distance. Once again, value can alter this effect.

Size influences depth. Because they are often the focal point in a quilt, small pieces seem to advance, especially when the color is intense. Large, expansive areas read as background and recede.

Placement affects depth. In an abstract composition, larger shapes placed near the lower edge appear closer, while smaller shapes placed higher seem distant, as in a landscape. Overlapping shapes enhance this illusion.

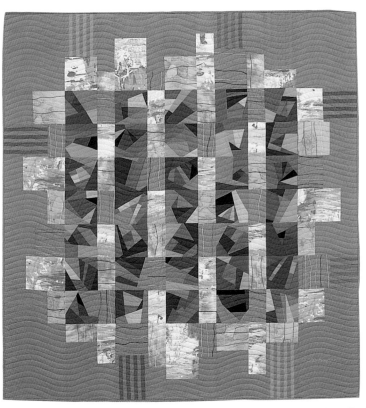

Daydreams *by Elaine Plogman, 1993, Cincinnati, Ohio, 48" x 50". (From the collection of Sara and David Plogman.) Brilliant colors set against a low-intensity background create depth and luminosity. To calm the intense colors in the Crazy quilt blocks, Elaine separated them with lighter-value mottled fabrics and low-intensity browns.*

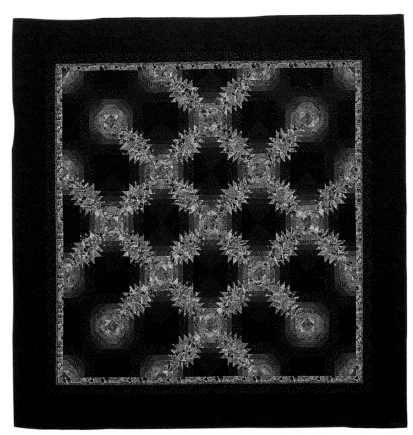

Carmen Miranda Meets American Gothic *by Christine A. Beck, 1995, Los Altos, California, 58" x 58". A light-value print with paper umbrellas was the color catalyst for this shimmering quilt. Gradated values of blue and violet play with the viewer's spatial perception, suggesting depth and luminosity.*

fabric

A love of fabric is what motivates quilters to make quilts, but with so many tempting choices, the pleasure can quickly turn into panic. Solids vary in color, value, and intensity, and these differences are obvious. Patterned fabrics, on the other hand, present more than a few challenges. A familiarity with pattern terms and styles will help you select and combine patterned fabrics with confidence.

A Pattern Vocabulary

You can describe patterned fabrics in terms of various design characteristics:

Motifs. These are the individual design elements in a pattern. A paisley is a motif; so is a squiggle in a contemporary design or a blossom in a floral print.

Ground color. This term refers to the color behind the motifs. When motifs are widely spaced, the ground color determines the overall color of the fabric.

Density. The spacing between motifs in a patterned fabric is known as density. Closely spaced designs tend to read as texture; open, airy patterns let the focus fall on the motifs.

Regular and irregular patterns. When motifs are consistent in orientation and spacing, the pattern is described as regular. In an irregular pattern, motifs are randomly scattered.

Repeats. A repeat is the distance from a point in one motif to the identical point in the next motif. If you plan to center motifs in block pieces, you'll need to consider the repeat when you calculate yardage.

One- and two-way patterns. In a one-way design, the motifs run in one direction; in a two-way design, they run both ways. Two-way patterns allow more flexibility in cutting.

Colorway. Now familiar to most quilters, the term colorway refers to the color scheme of a patterned fabric.

Pattern Scale

The size of the motifs or design lines in a pattern is known as scale. Pattern scale in fabric is usually described as small, medium, or large.

Small-scale patterns. Fabrics with small motifs are ideal for miniatures. As background pieces in larger quilts, small-scale patterns tend to read as solid color or subtle texture.

Small-, medium-, and large-scale patterns

Medium-scale patterns. These prints are versatile and easy to use because they retain their design, even from a distance, yet they rarely overpower the other fabrics.

Large-scale patterns. Large-scale prints are ideal candidates for selective cutting, but you must preview them carefully because they can appear fragmented when cut and sewn into blocks. Avoid using large-scale prints for small block pieces.

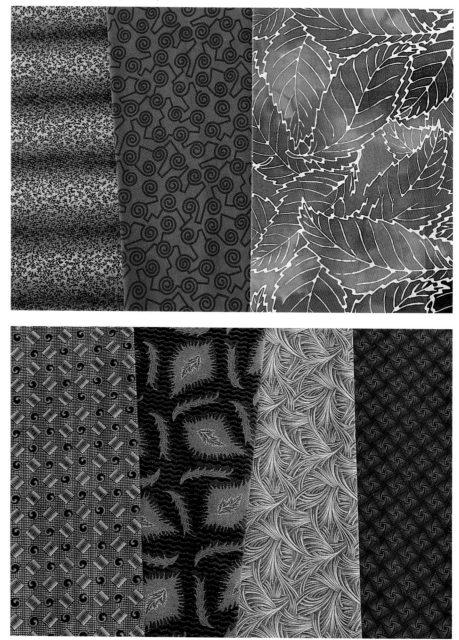

From left to right: a medium-density, two-way, regular pattern with distinct motifs on a variable ground color; an open, two-way, irregular pattern with a large repeat on a blue-and-black ground color; a dense, one-way, irregular pattern; a medium-density, two-way, regular pattern with a small repeat.

Pattern Styles

Pattern style, along with color, sets the mood of a fabric. Following are the most common pattern styles in quilting fabrics:

Representational. Realistic forms from nature, such as flowers, leaves, shells, and rocks, are known as representational patterns, but this category includes any realistic depiction of an object. Scenics make up a subcategory of representational patterns.

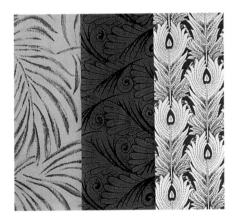

Stylized. Traditionally, stylized patterns simplify and repeat natural objects in a way that captures their essence. Some stylized patterns, such as the paisley, are classics; others convey a contemporary mood. It's often a fine line between representational and stylized patterns.

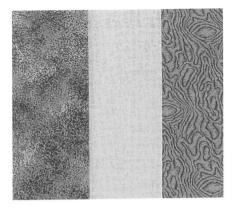

Near-solids. These patterns, sometimes called semi-solids, tend to read as solid color from a distance. Many are tone-on-tone, subtle variations of one or more closely related colors.

Geometric. This category includes designs based on lines, circles, or squares. Geometrics combine naturally with representational and stylized patterns when the fabrics have common colors.

Stripes and plaids. A subcategory of geometric, stripes and plaids provide a crisp contrast to curvilinear motifs.

Batik, painterly, and hand dyed. Mottled color and dappled light characterize these contemporary fabrics.

Abstract. Non-representational patterns that are neither stylized nor near-solid are sometimes called abstract.

Border prints. These specialized fabrics have a variety of uses in quilts. In addition to borders and sashing, they also work well in kaleidoscope blocks.

Novelty. Also known as conversational prints, novelty patterns depict real objects or living things, often in a humorous way.

Ethnic. Fabrics from different cultures mix easily with other patterns when they have common colors or related designs.

Transitional. Pattern styles that tie together or blend disparate fabrics are often referred to as transitional. These fabrics are frequently used for background pieces.

Pattern Combinations

How many times have you been surprised by the fabrics in a quilt? From a distance, the pieces are in perfect harmony, but up close, you find an incongruous, even jarring, collection of patterns. You ask yourself, "How did she know those fabrics would look so good together?"

She probably didn't, at least not until she auditioned them on her design wall or in sample blocks. You simply cannot predict how patterns will behave in each other's company until you see them together. What look like design enemies on bolts become kindred spirits when cut and pieced. To help you better combine patterns, consider what makes a quilt with patterned fabrics harmonious.

In classic design theory, harmony results when a design possesses both *variety* and *unity*. With the abundance of fabrics available to quilters, variety in pattern style is relatively easy to achieve. Take your cue from experienced quiltmakers and begin with more rather than fewer patterned fabrics. As you work on your design wall, you'll find it easier to eliminate fabrics that don't work than to add new ones to the group.

Varying the pattern scale of your fabrics is just as important as varying the style. If you've ever made a quilt with all medium-scale fabrics (perhaps it was your first), you understand the importance of variety in scale. You may want to err on the side of more, rather than less, variation in pattern scale because differences tend to diminish when you cut and piece fabrics.

Unity, the other half of the harmony equation, can be achieved through common colors, similar patterns, or an elusive quality known as

"pattern character," or pattern personality. Stylized florals and classic stripes, although different pattern styles, combine naturally because they share a traditional character. The same is true with a group of fabrics whose character is distinctly contemporary. On the other hand, a classic paisley may look out of place among splashy, abstract florals. Try to avoid personality conflicts among patterned fabrics, but don't play it too safe. When it comes to pattern, too much of the same thing is a recipe for a dull quilt. Remember the design equation: variety plus unity equals harmony.

Godey Design by Patrice Sims, 1996, Loomis, California. Unlikely patterns go together when they share colors. In this complex block, black and red are strong unifying factors.

Warm Path by Nancy Elliott MacDonald, 1992, Carmichael, California, 61" x 52". Prints and solids combine naturally when they share similar—but not identical—colors. Nancy began with leftovers, many of them hand-dyed fabrics, from an earlier quilt. To these she added two prints, one quiet, the other a large-scale floral print from Germany.

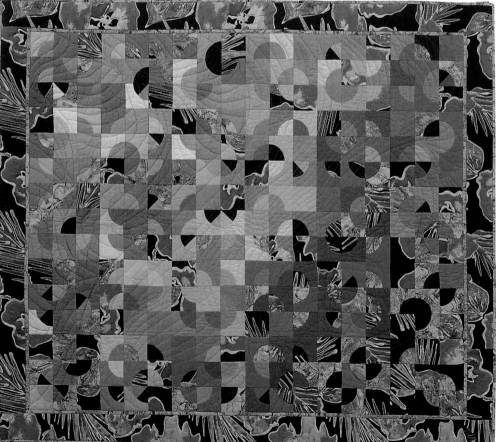

Texture

Two kinds of texture are relevant to quilters—actual texture and visual texture. Actual texture is the tactile quality that invites you to touch the surface of a fabric. Everyone enjoys the feel of fabric, but quiltmakers shy away from fabrics with actual texture because it's difficult to turn under or press open the seam allowances.

It is the actual texture made by quilting that enchants quilters and often proves irresistible to curious fingers at quilt shows. The miniature peaks and valleys created by quilting stitches lend subtle dimension to a quilt, visually blending and uniting the fabrics. Embellishments of all kinds—embroidery, beading, buttons, and so on—also contribute intriguing actual texture to quilts.

Visual texture is the look, rather than the feel, of a fabric. A rock-like pattern may appear rough, but of course, the fabric is smooth to the touch. All patterned fabrics, from representational to near-solid, possess visual texture.

Visual texture modulates color in powerful ways, especially from a distance. Imagine a medium-value, solid red fabric; then visualize the same red fabric with a dense squiggle pattern printed in black. The red that shows in the print is still medium in value, but the fabric reads as dark. In effect, your eye mixes the ground color and the black texture, producing a darker-value red.

Many hand-dyed and painterly fabrics are mottled or dappled, irregularities that read as subtle visual texture. Some hand-dyed fabrics are almost sueded, giving them a slight actual texture as well.

The guidelines that apply to pattern combinations also apply to texture. Variety in visual texture adds interest to a quilt, but too much variety can turn into visual chaos. Only by auditioning your fabrics can you find the right mix.

Texture plays a special role in background fabrics. Small-scale, low-contrast textures that read as solids or near-solids are ideal for the background pieces in a traditional quilt. For a background that unites and supports the main block pieces but does not compete with them, use a variety of similar but different textures, such as the mix of pale yellow prints in "Gypsy Crossroads" (page 100).

See page 87 in "A Color Workshop" for an exercise in pattern and texture.

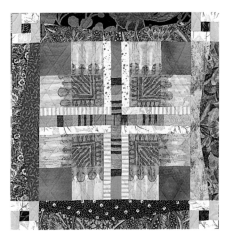

Varied patterns and textures enhance the mood of "African Crosses" (full quilt on page 78).

Ancient Graffiti by Charlotte Patera, 1995, Grass Valley, California, 48" x 48". To achieve the visual texture of primitive petroglyphs, Charlotte combined an assortment of contemporary prints and near-solids. The color scheme combines near-complementary blue-green and red with golds and browns.

A Fabric Collection

Fabric is to a quiltmaker what paint is to an artist. Like an artist, you need a complete, varied palette, but unlike an artist, you can't mix your colors—you must collect them as fabric. Whether you buy only what you need for a specific quilt or collect for your stash, finding the right fabrics is a challenge. Following are tips for building a well-rounded collection.

A Fabric Inventory

If you possess a "ton" of fabric, it's helpful to inventory your collection to see what you have. The easiest approach is to separate your fabric into stacks that correspond to the twelve hues on the color wheel, plus a stack for the true neutrals and the low-intensity colors that read as neutrals. Also create a stack for multi-colored prints that are difficult to classify.

Your stacks will no doubt vary in size, and the differences may reflect your color preferences. More likely, you don't have fabrics in certain colors because they aren't available—or weren't available when you wanted them. You may also have a greater number of medium and dark values than light. Light-value fabrics are more available than they were a few years ago, but medium and dark fabrics still predominate in many shops. Once you're aware of deficiencies in your collection, you can keep an eye out for the colors, values, intensities, and patterns you need.

Shopping Guidelines

Quilters hardly need shopping lessons, but a few guidelines may encourage more thoughtful buying and assuage any guilt you might have about your fabric stockpile.

"Buy early; buy often." For beginners and experienced quilters alike, a sound piece of advice on buying fabric is this: shop often and buy what you like, even if you don't know how you will use a fabric. Great fabrics come and go quickly, especially in busy quilt shops.

"Use your favorite fabrics." Quilters are sometimes reluctant to cut into special fabrics, but it's a good idea to use them while they still inspire you. If you keep making quilts, you'll probably outgrow the fabrics you currently love. Use your favorites now, and then buy new ones as you find them.

"A stash is a very good thing." If you choose to make quilts from the fabric you have on hand, you must—you must!—have a deep, diverse collection. In reality, most quilters work from their stashes and

A color inventory of your fabrics will reveal what you have and what you need to round out your stash.

out of a fabric, you can congratulate yourself for having used it up.

"Preview the possibilities." No matter how much experience you have, no matter how good you are at visualizing, fabric on bolts looks different once it's cut and pieced. To better anticipate how a fabric will look in a block, cut finished-size paper windows for each block piece, and then lay the windows on the fabrics you're considering. Or, frame a small area with L-shaped pieces of white paper. Be sure to stand back, squint, or use a reducing glass when you make your choices.

A Word to Beginners

If you have no quilts in your sewing history, you won't have a stash to dip into. Don't be discouraged—you can still make a beautiful quilt. Consider many different fabrics, but don't agonize over your choices; even experienced quilters buy fabrics they don't use.

Shop for fabric when you have time to experiment, and buy ⅛-yard cuts, if possible. As soon as you can, make a series of mock blocks (page 37), or sew a sample block to see if your fabrics work together; then return to buy the fabric you need. This approach lessens the chance of disappointment and motivates you to take the plunge.

buy new fabric as needed. You can't collect everything, and you can't find everything you need in one shopping trip. Unfortunately, some quilters don't stop buying what was once hard to find, even when it becomes plentiful. Others keep buying fabric for the quilts they just completed!

"There's safety in numbers." Here's another good excuse for collecting a wide variety of fabrics. If you make a quilt with five blue fabrics, any less-than-wonderful choices will broadcast their inadequacy. But if you use forty blues, mistakes will be lost in the crowd, and your eye will be pleasantly confused.

"Running out of fabric is never the disaster it seems." Running out forces you to make substitutions that will no doubt improve your quilt. Best of all, if you run

Paper windows and frames help you visualize how fabrics will look in a block.

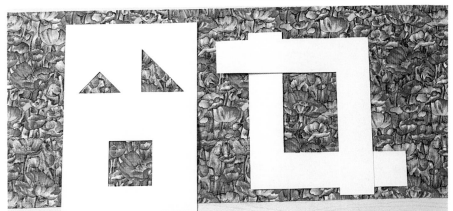

The Cast of Fabrics

Fabrics play different roles in a quilt design, much like actors in a play. You might even think of your fabrics as the cast. One fabric takes the lead, several have supporting roles, while others put in cameo appearances. Prospective cast members go through the all-important audition, and once chosen, the ensemble tells a story or carries out a theme.

The lead fabric: a starring role. Many quiltmakers, beginners and veterans alike, begin with a lead, or focus, fabric, and then add fabrics to complete the scheme. This approach has advantages, but there are hazards. Here's how to make this time-honored strategy work for you:

Start with a drop-dead-fabulous fabric, one that you absolutely love. Look for a multi-colored print with a variety of values. (A range of values makes it easy to go lighter and darker with your supporting fabrics.) For the most flexibility, choose a fabric with a medium- or large-scale pattern. A large-scale pattern allows you to cut pieces from different areas for different effects, but the pattern may look fragmented if your pieces are small. Be sure to preview potential fabrics to anticipate any problems.

If you never use your lead fabric—and many quilters have more than a few had-to-have-it fabrics sitting on their shelves—don't feel guilty. It has served its purpose if it inspires you to go in a different direction or simply pleases you.

Supporting-role fabrics. Your lead fabric may be stunning, but it's the supporting-role fabrics that make or break your quilt. To select the best supporting fabrics, look to your lead fabric for color cues. What are the color relationships? Which colors predominate? In what proportions do they occur? As you answer these questions about your lead fabric, begin to assemble your supporting cast:

1. Pull bolts or pieces of fabric that match the colors in the lead fabric. This step is easy for everyone.

A red-violet and orange batik inspires a cast of related and contrasting fabrics. Yellow-greens complement the red-violet. Lighter blues echo the nearly navy blue in the lead fabric.

2. Next, pull fabrics that vary slightly in color, value, and intensity. Go lighter and darker, brighter and duller, and don't be afraid to wander around the color wheel and choose colors that are a bit off. If your lead fabric contains rose (a medium-value red), for example, introduce a fabric that you might describe as claret (a dark-value red-violet). In a nutshell, vary the colors, values, and intensities slightly from those in your lead fabric.

If you use your lead fabric as the color catalyst for a scheme, but don't plan to include it in your quilt, go ahead and pull supporting fabrics that match the lead. Variations will keep the scheme from looking overmatched.

When choosing supporting fabrics, quilters sometimes focus so much on color that they unconsciously choose near-solids. Strive for variety in pattern and texture; otherwise, your quilt will read as a mix of patterned and solid fabrics, an effect you may not like.

3. With what you know about color relationships, can you introduce a new color or colors to the cast? If your lead fabric has analogous blues and violets, for example, try adding a touch of yellow-orange, the complement of blue-violet. Suddenly, your analogous scheme becomes a split complement. If your lead is predominantly peach and green, bring in accents of pink and blue to make a double split complement of pink (a tint of red) and green, and peach (a tint of orange) and blue.

4. Now—this is the test—take your lead fabric out of the group, step back, and analyze your cast. Can they stand alone, or do they collapse visually? If your supporting fabrics possess sufficient variety in color, value, intensity, scale, and pattern, they will look good together, even without the lead fabric.

One way to ensure a strong cast is to introduce one or more supporting fabrics that are just as powerful as your lead fabric. In other words, make them co-stars.

Background fabrics: a key role. The relationship between the foreground and background fabrics in a quilt is a special one, requiring special consideration.

In traditional quilts, such as "Irish Chain" (page 65) and "Tennessee Waltz" (page 69), a light, neutral background supports and unites darker, more colorful blocks. You can use the same neutral background fabric throughout, or you can use a variety of related background fabrics, placing them randomly across the quilt. In "Free As a Bird" (page 107), thirty-five neutral background fabrics create the impression of light skipping across the quilt surface.

Near-solid or tone-on-tone neutrals are favorite background fabrics in traditional quilts, but also consider subtle plaids, stripes, and textures in low-contrast values and quiet colors.

When you want to use a colored background, look to your cast for color cues. In a quilt with blue, blue-violet, violet, and green appliqué, for example, buttery yellow is a good candidate for the background because it is a component of green (yellow and blue make green) and the complement of violet.

In contemporary quilts, the background is often delightfully ambiguous, echoing foreground colors or subtly merging different planes. "Kaleidoscopic XIII: Random Acts of Color" and "AutoFiction: Building Blocks" (page 77) feature backgrounds that play an integral role in the design.

Accent fabrics: a cameo appearance. Accent fabrics, or "zingers" as they're sometimes called, can lighten and brighten a quilt. Quilters often choose an intense color for the accent, but softer, duller colors, such as cinnamon and brick, are effective in low-intensity schemes. Many quilters swear by yellow as an accent color. "Every quilt needs a little yellow" was heard at show-and-tell for several years. Yellow is a wonderful accent color because it is naturally light in value and visually warm.

How much of an accent is enough and how much is overkill? It depends, but in general, the brighter the accent, the less you will want to see. If even small pieces of an accent fabric overpower a quilt design, search for a fabric that contains the accent color, such as a violet floral with splashes of yellow.

A final word of encouragement about the process of selecting a cast of fabrics: At some point in your quiltmaking career, your experience will kick in, and choosing a successful group of fabrics will become easier. You must grow to this point; it rarely happens all at once. So keep at it—the quilt you are making now is practice for your next one.

Tropical fish on a pale yellow ground portray a triad of blue-green, red-violet, and yellow-orange. A painterly gray print and yellow near-solid provide light values.

Color and Value Strategies

"I have no trouble choosing fabrics—I just don't know where to put them" is a common complaint among quilters, especially beginners. Following are several time-tested color and value strategies.

Repeat-Fabric Blocks

In recent years, the trend has been away from quilts that use the same fabrics in each block to quilts that use different fabrics in the blocks. But the simple repeat-fabric approach is still a good one, especially for a beginner with a limited stash. When the cast of fabrics is sensational, repeat-fabric blocks possess a simplicity and rhythm not always found in multi-fabric quilts.

To enhance the interest in a repeat-fabric quilt, use fabrics with more rather than fewer colors, and include an assortment of pattern styles and scales. A block with as many pieces as you can handle is a good choice because it requires a greater variety of fabrics.

Multi-Fabric Blocks

Quilts with blocks made of different fabrics have a spontaneity and vitality prized by quilters and quilt admirers. You can visually unite the blocks in multi-fabric quilts by repeating the colors or the values from block to block. Here's how:

- Repeat the colors, but vary the fabrics. Quilts in this category feature the same colors in the same positions in each block, but different fabrics. Using different fabrics ensures slight variations in color, value, intensity, and texture that make a multi-fabric quilt so appealing. This color-driven approach is ideal for the quilter who has a good collection of fabrics in each color family.
- Repeat the values, but vary the fabrics. The blocks in "Stars Out of Africa" (above right) illustrate the value-driven approach to a quilt plan. The fabrics vary

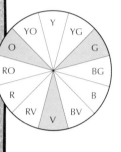

Value is a unifying element in "Stars Out of Africa." The fabrics vary, but the relative values repeat from block to block. This strategy is most successful when the fabrics have a similar character.

throughout the quilt, but the block pieces maintain the same value relationships—dark star centers, light surrounding triangles, dark star points, and light background. The overall effect is sophisticated and harmonious.

You can, of course, combine both variables in one quilt, repeating the colors and the relative values, but varying the fabrics from block to block. "Gypsy Crossroads" repeats both the colors and values in an assortment of compatible, yet varied, fabrics.

The fabrics vary widely in "Gypsy Crossroads," but the blocks maintain the same color and value relationships: dark-value violet fabrics for the foreground triangles, and light-value yellow fabrics for the background.

color stories

A square-in-a-square design lends itself to a colorful cast of supporting fabrics.

Every quilt tells a color story, and it often begins with a block design and a great cast of fabrics. On the following pages, you'll find the step-by-step evolution of one color scheme, followed by six short color stories. In the next chapter, two quilters tell the color and design stories behind their outstanding quilts.

A Way to Work: Balkan Puzzle

Quilters have their favorite ways of working. Some can't wait to get their hands on their fabrics and start a quilt, without making even one sample block. Others like to audition fabrics and make sample blocks slowly and painstakingly, until they're completely satisfied with their choices. What follows is a compromise strategy, a fast, fun way to play with the possibilities without wasting valuable time or fabric. Follow the process, mistakes included, as a color story unfolds.

Getting Started

This color scheme begins with a variation of the Balkan Puzzle block and a tropical print whose main colors are intense, complementary red-orange and blue-green, with various blues, greens, reds, oranges, and yellows. It's not a quilting fabric, but the colors are rich and varied, and it looks like an ideal lead fabric.

The supporting fabrics key off the colors in the lead fabric but don't match them: a red-orange (more red than orange) near-solid in a pattern that looks like molten lava; a red painterly print with spatters of orange; the same painterly print in blue with spatters of blue-green; a mottled green leaf print with overtones of blue. Light-value green and blue-green fabrics balance the medium-to-dark values in the lead fabric. A dappled yellow-green tree print looks like the perfect background.

Working with the Block Design

Experimenting with the block before you even think about where you'll place your fabrics helps you see your design options without the distraction of color.

1. Begin by drawing multiples of the block on graph paper that has four squares per inch. To make this task easy, draw the blocks at one-fourth scale; that is, one small square for each inch in your block.

2. Cut the paper blocks apart and arrange them in various settings—straight, on point, with plain alternate blocks, with pieced alternate blocks, etc. (Using a removable-adhesive gluestick makes rearranging the blocks easy.) As you work, search for strong design lines and secondary patterns.

3. Once you're satisfied with the setting, photocopy it at a reduced size for coloring. Working small cuts down on coloring time and allows you to see different effects quickly.

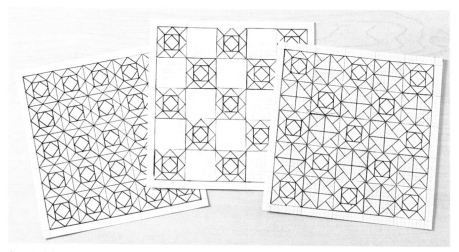

In a straight set of repeat blocks, pinwheels form where the blocks meet. Plain alternate blocks open up the design. Pieced alternate blocks preserve the corner triangles.

Working with Value and Color

Now it's time to add value and color to the equation. Shade or color several versions of your chosen setting using gray or colored pencils. Some quiltmakers use only gray pencils to develop pure value relationships; others prefer colored pencils and manipulate the value by varying the pressure or relying on the inherent value of the colors. (Yellow-orange, for example, is naturally lighter than blue-violet.) The choice is yours.

There are, of course, numerous ways to use this cast of fabrics in a Balkan Puzzle block. The lead fabric, selectively cut, is an obvious choice for the center square. Surrounding the lead fabric with alternating cool and warm colors ensures balance in visual temperature, with an emphasis on the cool hues.

When colored, the straight setting reveals a value/color weakness: where the red-orange triangles touch the blue triangles, the pieces run together, in part because the values are similar. There's only one way to tell if the color plan will work, and that's by testing it with fabric.

A straight set presents more than a few design challenges, all related to value and intensity.

Working with Your Fabrics

The real fun begins when you start cutting and positioning your fabrics. If you are brave and have lots of fabric, consider cutting actual-size pieces, including seam allowances, and developing your blocks on your design wall. When you're happy with the design, you're set to sew. If you go this route, cut a variety of fabrics so you'll have many different pieces to play with; save the ones that don't work for another quilt.

Mock Blocks

You can also make mock blocks to see how your fabrics work in combination before you cut actual pieces. To make a mock block, draw your block on graph paper and make at least four photocopies. Then, cut finished-size pieces of fabric to fit the block and compose one block on your design wall, moving and substituting pieces until you're happy with the design. Glue the pieces to the pattern and trim the excess.

Make at least four mock blocks to see how the colors and shapes interact, especially where the blocks meet. If you're not satisfied with a few of your fabric choices, cut new pieces and lay them on top of the first pieces; they will stick, just as they do to flannel or fleece.

Mock blocks can be any size. Full-size blocks show you exactly how your blocks will appear, but they use the most fabric. To save fabric, make 6" mock blocks for 9" finished blocks, or 9" mock blocks for 12" finished blocks.

At this point you may be thinking that you don't want to make mock blocks—they sound like a waste of time and fabric. Try to see it another way: You're not wasting fabric—you're using it. And by taking the time to explore all the color and design options, you'll have a better quilt in the end. It's always worth it.

The red-orange triangles advance, but so do the blue triangles.

Where the red-orange and blue triangles touch, the near-complementary colors vibrate.

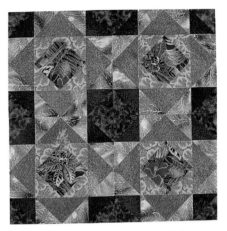

Separating the intense colors makes all the difference.

Four Balkan Puzzle mock blocks illustrate what can happen when you translate a color study into fabric:

1. The first block starts with a selectively cut square of the lead fabric, surrounded by light-value blue-green triangles and intense red-orange triangles. The blue painterly print and the tree print become the corner triangles. The problem that surfaced at the colored-pencil stage occurs: the red-orange and blue fabrics are too close in value, and the pieces don't visually separate.

2. In a group of four mock blocks, the red-orange and blue triangles merge and fight for attention. There's also an unpleasant effect of simultaneous contrast (page 24) where the intense, near-complementary colors touch. It's difficult to read the overall pattern.

3. Changing the corner pieces to separate the red-orange and blue fabrics resolves the problem. Suddenly, the Balkan Puzzle blocks become Connecticut blocks (pages 40–41). The red-orange units advance, and the surrounding green reads as a light, airy background. Where the four blocks meet, a subtle secondary pattern forms. The design has evolved considerably from the original concept, but it works, and that's the goal.

Vibrant Amish Star

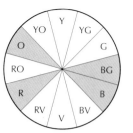

1. Four Anvil blocks form the block known as Amish Star. A red-and-black print serves as the lead fabric. Blues and oranges in a variety of values and intensities make the scheme complementary; blue-green prints soften the contrast.

2. The lead fabric, with its grid design, is ideal for the center square; intense blue star points provide brightness. The pointillist and painterly prints echo the center star.

3. A speckled, more intense blue-green print holds its own with the other fabrics and adds needed texture to the block.

4. Where the four blocks meet, ghosted stars form, with just a hint of transparency. The star points connect to form diagonal chains that are bright, then ghosted, then bright again.

Sweet Amish Star

1. Complementary pinks and greens in a variety of values, intensities, patterns, and textures tell an entirely different color story. Accents of yellow-orange in the darkest green print provide a color cue for one of the background fabrics.

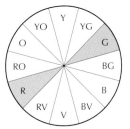

2. Dark green points and various 1930s or "lipstick" pink squares make up the main star. In the corners, the colors reverse: dark pink points and light green squares. The light-value background fabrics add soft color and texture to the scheme.

3. A new print—this one red, not pink— placed between the star points advances against the background and strengthens the diagonal link between the stars.

4. From a distance, the background prints fool the eye and blend to form a new, ambiguous color—is it peach, pink, or yellow? A ghosted star forms where the blocks meet, but the chain is less pronounced because the colors are reversed.

Enigmatic Connecticut

1. The square-in-a-square format is ideal for experimenting with transparency (page 23). Complementary red-violet and yellow-green provide a place to begin; a yellow-orange stripe batik and a multi-colored print and plaid add variety to the scheme.

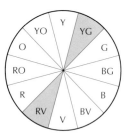

2. The stripe surrounding the center square adds warmth, but it is too bright and too solid in relation to the red-violet batik to make a convincing transparency. The green triangles are too similar in value.

3. Triangles cut from lighter areas of the red-violet batik are more effective; so is a plain yellow-orange batik. It now looks as though a large square of yellow-orange rests on top of four red-violet rectangles. A hand-dyed green fabric dappled with light enhances the transparency.

4. Four blocks read as transparent, on-point squares floating above a dark red-violet background. Bits of blue and violet in the multi-colored print bring the scheme closer to a double split complement of red-violet, yellow-green, blue-violet, and yellow-orange.

Classic Connecticut

1. A triad of low-intensity primaries (red, blue, and yellow) presents a design challenge. Because the fabrics lack brilliance, variety in value is essential. A touch of green (a classic addition to a triad of primaries) cools the scheme.

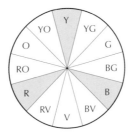

2. The blue triangles and surrounding red triangles merge, diminishing the impact of the design. The block needs more value contrast. Even with the green, the visual temperature feels too warm.

3. Surrounding the blue triangles with the pinstripe lightens the block and gives it dimension. A light-value red print frames the center square, bringing even more light to the design. Yellow accents in the prints maintain the triad.

4. The blue on-point squares appear to float on the pinstripe background. Where the blocks meet, a secondary pattern of Broken Dishes forms. The design is crisp, balanced, and uncluttered.

Autumn Churn Dash

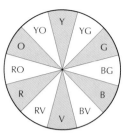

1. A multicolored batik offers a wealth of color cues. Hand-dyed solids echo the colors and visual texture of the lead fabric. Smoldering versions of primary and secondary colors mingle on a mixed-color ground.

2. Light and dark versions of low-intensity violet key off the colors in the center square, but the rectangles and square merge because the values are similar. A bright yellow background complements the violets.

3. A paler, less demanding yellow background recedes, focusing attention on the positive-space shapes. Cutting the rectangles and triangles from complementary colors better emphasizes the block design.

4. Complements used in equal quantities don't fight when the colors are low in intensity. Traditional sashing separates and unifies the blocks.

Oceany Churn Dash

1. A traditional interpretation of the Churn Dash block calls for only three or four fabrics. A watery blue-green and red-violet batik looks like an ideal background fabric. Two leaf prints, one also a batik, have the visual weight necessary for the foreground shapes.

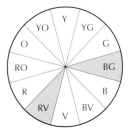

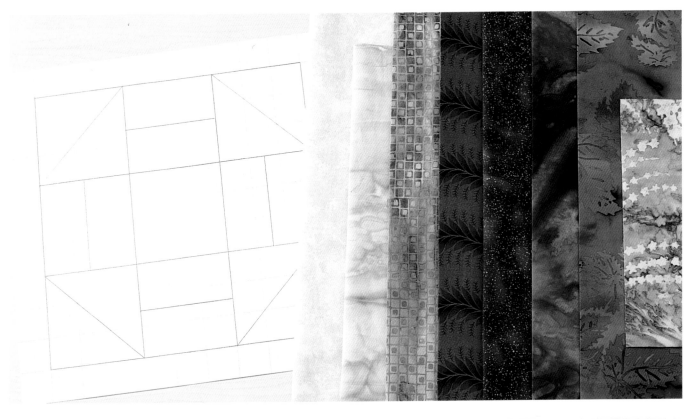

2. The block lacks the variety needed in a two-color scheme. The batik looks fragmented when cut up for the background, and the values are too similar.

3. A batik in lighter versions of the same two colors, with touches of near-white, brings the block to life. A hand-dyed fabric for the center square adds to the sense of depth.

4. Pale sashing spaces out the blocks. Variations in the background fabric enhance the visual interest. Touches of yellow-orange would turn this two-color scheme into a triad of intermediates (page 19).

Many prints make their way into Ruth's quilt, among them representational, stylized, geometric, batik, and near-solid. Most are contemporary; a few are reproduction fabrics. From left to right: fabrics for the inner compass points, outer compass points, and fleur de lis appliqué.

Between the Devil and the Deep Blue Sea

Ruth Cattles Cottrell

My interpretation of the classic Mariner's Compass design is the result of an ongoing infatuation with antique quilts. I was inspired by an article in *Folk Art Magazine* (Winter 1994) that featured an exquisite Mariner's Compass quilt by Emeline Barker, a quiltmaker who lived in New York. Made in the late 1800s, Emeline's quilt is a masterpiece of piecing, appliqué, and quilting. My goal was to capture the spirit of this breathtaking quilt using all new fabrics.

Value is the key to successfully replicating a historic quilt. If the values are right, just about anything works in terms of color. I use my red filter to analyze potential fabrics for value, and I am sometimes surprised by what it reveals.

In the original quilt, the compass points were red, green, blue, and brown, a combination I wanted to maintain. I decided to use a different red and green fabric in each compass but to keep the blue and brown fabrics constant throughout. For almost every pair of fabrics, I chose a red that is lighter in value than the green. The red compass points appear to advance, thanks to their placement and value.

Finding the right combination of blue and brown fabrics for the remaining compass points proved to be a bigger challenge. My first choices, a blue-and-black print and a brown print, read as the same dark value when I made a test wedge and looked at it through my filter. I had hoped to create a sense of outward movement in each compass, but this combination of fabrics didn't give the effect I wanted.

Off to the quilt shop I went. This time I selected a large-scale, blue-and-brown batik. Those in the shop thought my choice was a mistake, but I saw potential in this fabric's lighter values and mottled colors, and I was confident that it would lose its contemporary look when cut up. I was right; this very modern fabric, which is so far from the fabrics in the original quilt, brings light and movement to each compass.

I took my inspiration for the quilting from Emeline's quilt as well. For the small circle around each compass and between the fleur de lis motifs, I used a quarter to mark the design.

Between the Devil and the Deep Blue Sea *by Ruth Cattles Cottrell, 1996, Irving, Texas, 72" x 72".*
The blue fish batik used for the corner wedges inspired the quilt title. In seafaring lore, the "devil" was the ship's molding near the water line. When a sailor was lowered to remove the barnacles from the molding, he was said to be "between the devil and the deep blue sea."

Feelin' Fine

Elaine Plogman

If ever there was "feel good" music, it is zydeco, the popular Cajun music of southern Louisiana. Listening to the bayou tunes while choosing fabrics for a new quilt, I was caught up in the lilting rhythms. The music took possession of the process, and the result is a quilt that nearly dances off the wall.

For some time I had wanted to make a quilt using a Star block I had designed and a growing collection of my own hand-dyed, hand-painted, and airbrushed fabrics. To these I added a variety of commercial abstract prints and textures.

For every quilt I make, I do a value study using gray pencils. I think quilters skip an important step when they go straight from quilt idea to cutting and sewing. They can't wait to get to their fabrics, but it's well worth the time it takes to sketch a quilt design. I use an average of five values in a sketch, assigning a specific lightness or darkness to each shape in a block. The closer I stick to my value study, the more successful the quilt is.

"Feelin' Fine" displays a fairly limited palette of blue, orange, red, and green (a double split complement), plus neutrals. I repeated the relative values but varied the colors from block to block. Solids and near-solids help tame the multitude of prints. The intense strip-pieced "wings" and low-intensity borders echo the colors and values of the blocks.

I initially designed the Star block to stand alone in a small wall quilt, and I chose the values accordingly. When I made multiple blocks and arranged them on my design wall, they read as sixteen separate units, with no connecting element. Each block begged to be framed, and the top as a whole needed some zip. To liven things up, I made narrow sashing using leftovers from the wings. I decided not to square up the 11" x 12" blocks and instead rotated and stair-stepped them to make the surface jump. Small squares of color and hand-embroidered squiggles link the border and the blocks.

An incongruous mix of prints, solids, and hand-created fabrics becomes a beautiful blend of color and pattern in "Feelin' Fine."

Feelin' Fine by Elaine Plogman, 1995, Cincinnati, Ohio, 59" x 59". Elaine puts the principles of good design to work in this lively quilt. The colors vary across the quilt, but the values repeat from block to block, unifying the quilt through repetition.

avoiding the pitfalls

Who hasn't looked at a just-completed quilt and thought, "I wish I had…"? All quilters, even the most accomplished, make color choices they later regret. If you're unhappy with a quilt you have made, try to determine the problem. If you're planning a quilt, now is the time to anticipate and troubleshoot mistakes. Following are common color and design pitfalls and ways to remedy or avoid them.

Color

"I love teal and magenta, but I'm stuck in a rut."

If you adore certain colors and find yourself repeating them quilt after quilt, look to your color wheel for new color cohorts. What's the third leg in a triad of teal (blue-green) and magenta (red-violet)? Yellow-orange. You probably won't want to make a quilt with an abundance of yellow-orange, but an accent of "mango" or another warm color might be just the spark teal and magenta need.

Investigate other color schemes that include teal. Consider complementary teal (blue-green) and coral (red-orange), accented by carnation (a tint of red) and melon (a tint of orange), the two colors adjacent to red-orange on the color wheel. And don't be afraid to include colors that add a little—just a little—tension to your quilt design.

In defense of those quilters content to be stuck in a color warp, there is no rule that says you can't make what pleases you, even if it's another peach and green quilt. After all, it's your time and fabric. It's your quilt. But do try for more color variety. To peach and green, for example, you might add violet, which turns the two-color scheme into a triad of secondaries.

"It hurts to look at my quilt."

When a quilt makes you cringe, the cause is often an imbalance in visual temperature or an excess of intense color. A quilt that contains only blues, greens, and violets can look cold and uninviting. An all-orange quilt, on the other hand, is likely to agitate both the maker and the viewer. When you work with colors from the same side of the color wheel, balance the visual temperature with doses of complementary color. Neutrals and low-intensity colors also provide welcome visual relief in strong schemes.

Using your colors in equal quantities can be another source of visual discomfort. Look to your lead fabric for help in determining a pleasing ratio of colors.

"Even with the color wheel, I need help choosing colors."

Decorating textiles are a wonderful source of color cues. Start with a color you like or want to use in your quilt, then search for decorating fabrics or other textiles that contain the color. Note the combination of colors and their relationship on the color wheel and try to adapt them to your quilt design. If your key color is red-orange, for example, an embroidered pillow with blues, greens, and corals might inspire you. (This combination consists of a split complement of blue, green, and red-orange.) Or, notice that terra cotta and olive green are balanced by accents of blue in an ethnic rug. (This combination is a near triad of red-orange, yellow-green, and blue.) Tapestries and plaids also display visually delicious color combinations that can be adapted to quilts.

Value and Intensity

"My fabrics run together, and the design is flat."

The problem probably lies with value. It's a challenge to find that magical mix of light, medium, and dark values. Fabrics that appear distinctly different in value on the bolt can blend when cut and sewn into a block. Try using one of the value-determining tools or techniques (see Tip on page 7) to help you choose fabrics with sufficient light-and-dark contrast.

"One piece pops out—it's the first thing I see."

If a piece stands out, there is probably too much contrast in value, either between pieces or in the piece itself. Dark prints with white motifs or design lines are common offenders. If you're devoted to a high-contrast fabric, consider overdyeing it to lower the value and take the edge off the contrast. An intense color may also come forward, especially if it's surrounded by low-intensity colors.

"My quilt looks washed out."

If you take your color cues from your lead fabric but ignore the design lines, which are usually dark and contrasting, your quilt may look faded. Study your lead and supporting fabrics, and if they contain dark colors, even as design lines, include a few dark-value fabrics as accents.

A quilt that includes only low- or medium-intensity colors is also likely to look washed out. Accents of intense color can bring a dull scheme to life.

Variety

"It's overmatched."

If your quilt looks like one piece of fabric, you haven't pushed your colors far enough. Review the guidelines on pages 32–33 for choosing lead and supporting fabrics that go beyond the obvious. Including transition colors that lie between the colors in your lead fabric is one way to expand a combination. If your lead fabric contains red and blue, for example, a violet fabric may be just what your scheme needs.

By the way, no fair pulling fabrics in colors that match exactly the registration dots on the selvage. If you do, your quilt is likely to look overmatched. The registration dots can, however, provide valuable color hints. You may not realize that a brown print contains a deep, dark red until you see the dot of red on the selvage. In this case, you might add a dark red to your cast or audition other dark-value colors.

"It's still boring."

Even when you include a mix of values, intensities, patterns, and textures, a quilt can lack vitality. Your design may need an element of color surprise. Introduce the complement of your main color, such as an accent of celadon (yellow-green) in a scheme that is predominantly magenta (red-violet).

Another solution to the predictability problem is to use a greater variety of fabrics, which will naturally bring bits of unexpected color, pattern, and texture to your quilt design.

"My lead fabric takes over!"

This mistake is common when you build a cast of fabrics that is obviously subordinate to the lead. Try adding a few supporting fabrics whose patterns are the same scale as the pattern in your lead fabric.

Design

"It's chaotic."

This problem often occurs when you cut large-scale fabrics into small pieces. Consider carefully the size of your pieces when you choose patterned fabrics. Too much strong color in a quilt, without a place for the eye to rest, also contributes to a sense of visual chaos.

"My mock blocks looked great, but the quilt is disappointing."

You probably failed to step back far enough when you auditioned your fabrics and made your mock blocks. What works up close doesn't necessarily work at a distance, and what doesn't work up close may look great at a distance. Stand back!

"I'm stuck, and I don't have a clue about what to do."

Hit the books—quilt books, that is. Ask great quilters what they do for inspiration, and many will tell you that they pore over their quilt books. Look for color cues in quilts that you like: What colors did the quiltmaker use and in what proportion? Are the quilts balanced in terms of color temperature? Is there a broad or narrow range of values and intensities? Analyzing and critiquing old and new quilts improves your color and design skills. Be patient with the process.

"It's hopeless."

Sometimes you must throw in the quilt, so to speak. But before you do, try once more to understand and remedy the problem. Often a solution will appear just when you think there is none. A background fabric that's just a little lighter transforms a dreary block into a radiant one; a slightly different red sets a shape apart from its neighbors. You may be only one fabric away from a quilt that you love.

Borders

"I don't have enough of the fabric I wanted to use for the border. Now what?"

If you can't use one of your block fabrics for the border, relax; a new fabric may be even better for your quilt. Just be sure to choose one that relates to the colors and patterns in your block fabrics. Many quilters routinely use a different fabric for the border. In fact, they don't even think about the border until the blocks are finished.

A narrow inner border acts much like the inner mat on a framed picture. This border is the perfect place to use accent colors. An inner border can also bridge the gap between the blocks and the outer border.

"When I added the border, my quilt died."

When a border drags down a quilt, differences in intensity and fabric character are often to blame. Even if the colors are harmonious, a low-intensity border can kill a group of intense blocks.

"The fabric I chose for the border overwhelms my blocks."

Chances are, the problem lies with the scale of your border fabric. A border is meant to complete the blocks, not compete with them. One way to guarantee a harmonious relationship between the border and blocks in a traditional quilt is to use the background fabric for the border.

For a border that's different from the background, start the auditioning process with a fabric that is slightly darker in value than the average value of the blocks. If that fabric doesn't work, audition lighter and darker fabrics until you find one that enhances the blocks. Beware of borders that are too dark; they tend to trap the blocks.

quilters on color

Wendy Hill

Nurturing the Vision

Color is described scientifically as wavelengths of light, but to me it is a magical gateway to the world of images and ideas. I think and remember in color; I dream in color; I imagine in color. As a girl I loved opening a new box of crayons and staring at the seventy-odd pointed cylinders of color lined up in rows. I grew up drawing, painting, gardening, and sewing, yet color was the real medium I explored.

Each of my quilts starts with an idea. I store images and thoughts until one day something new forms, and a vision is born. For "The River of Dreams," I saw in my

Funny Side Up, 1992, 33" x 33". In response to a challenge competition with a food theme, Wendy designed and made this colorful tribute to the lowly fried egg. To bring movement to the design, she strip-pieced a portion of each block, and then rotated the blocks. Trapunto yolks made of lamé stand out and shine against low-intensity egg "whites."

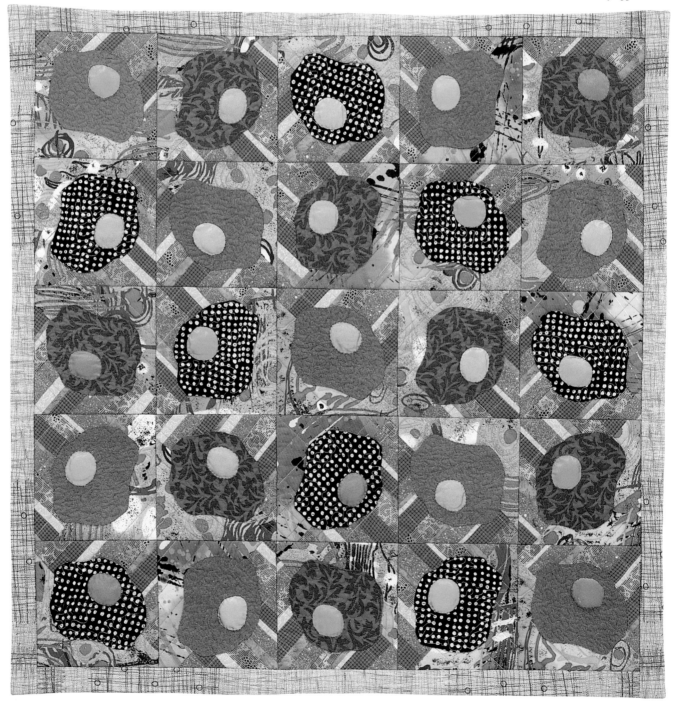

The River of Dreams, *1995, 37" x 37". To interpret her watery vision, Wendy wove raw-edge strips on the diagonal, leaving some to dangle from the lower edge. Coral (a tint of red-orange) complements the cool greens, blue-greens, and blues.*

vision, and collecting fabric is the most enjoyable part of the design process. I seek out fabrics that go with my vision and bring out the best in each other. Fabric by itself has certain attributes—color, pattern, texture, scale, and so on. But when fabrics are combined, they come alive with properties relative to each other, such as light/dark, soft/harsh, bright/dull, advancing/receding. A fabric that looks awful in one group of fabrics may shine in another.

Each of us has a unique way of developing an idea into a quilt, yet there are strategies anyone can use to make the process more fluent and effective. One approach that works for me is to collect fabric for a specific quilt rather than to buy in general. Before I shop, I jot down notes about the kinds of colors, textures, and scales I hope to find in fabric. Outside the store I review my notes, and then I boldly walk in prepared for the onslaught to my senses. After each purchase, I glue a snippet of the fabric to my note sheet, which slowly blooms into a wonderful color chart.

Buying fabrics over a period of time allows me to get just the right pieces without feeling pressured. In a sense, I audition my fabrics as I buy them. I experience in my mind how fabrics will work with my vision: this piece will lead me to the image I want to express; that piece won't take me there. A few fabrics don't make it into the final mix, but for the most part, the choices are made before I begin the quilt.

Nurturing a vision and finding fabrics that fulfill it has helped me to build color confidence and to hone my skills. With practice, the process becomes seamless, and the vision that began with a glimpse or a memory turns into a tangible expression of images and ideas.

Wendy Hill lives in Sunriver, Oregon.

mind's eye a cold, crisp, wet scene that included the texture of water flowing over thick plants, with a flash of fish just under the surface. My vision included images of salmon circling a hatchery tank, a grate at the bottom of a pool of water, a picture of migrating carp. From a collection of vague and clear memories, I make the leap from idea to vision.

Next I analyze my vision. I want to exploit the idea and push its limits. Asking "What if?" questions helps me to develop my vision into a quilt others can see too. I try out different approaches in my mind or in quick drawings, all the time narrowing down the options for color, texture, line, scale, fabric, technique, and size.

Color is an essential element of my

Joan Colvin

Naturally Inspired

I care about color, and I am constantly aware of the scene before me—the time of day, the time of year, the quality of the light. The blueberry bushes in winter are redder through my sunglasses, the potato blossoms more lavender each day of summer. I have a white flower garden, more or less to see how many kinds of white I can find and to enjoy the foliage, multicolored by contrast. For the house, I find just the right shade of warm gray for the door frames. Where I have a choice, I must get it right. Since what is right is so personal, I can only urge you to indulge your inclinations.

In first and second grades, the watercolor boxes passed around in art class were generally muddied and nearly empty of red, blue, and green. So you were on your own with yellow, purple, black, and whatever residue you could flood out with your brush. Maybe my relaxation with shades and tones started there. Art class was joyous, and you took what you could get.

I am at ease with nature's quiet hues, yet I appreciate the power of saturated color. Remember Piglet, rolling home after a bath in order to get a comfortable color? Am I like that? I can play at my working wall for some time, making what seem like major color changes, substituting and shifting. But, standing back, the piece is gray and oatmeal—has been and always will be. I remind myself to throw in tiny bits of wild color, just to make a livelier gray.

Occasionally I am captured by a wonderful fabric that gleams and glistens with color and texture. This becomes a keynote fabric, and all else flows from it. The fabric demands decisions: Are the colors to be featured? Do I pull out certain ones and use lots? In this way the keynote piece is a stepping-stone to a fuller statement. Or, does the keynote piece stand out grandly (or subtly), needing only a nudge here and there and a supporting cast, of neutrals perhaps, to allow it to star?

Alders, *1995, 42" x 70". On first impression, Joan's composition of intermeshing marshland and trees says "monochromatic," but her palette is in fact rich and diverse. Tans and golds warm up inky blue and dark rose hues; a wide assortment of textures and values sets the scene.*

It's nice if this process can be intuitive. Just when I think mine is, and I can speed along, I find myself needing to try out my combinations, one by one, value by value. "This is OK," I say to myself. "This is better; this is out. Whoa! This is it, the best so far!" I don't think about the components of the colors I want. Instead, I think vivid; bright; softer; related to this but warmer; a touch of cool that doesn't match; not so flat and solid; a mix of this and that for transition. I grab from my stash, much as I might splash in jars of paint. Good things

Silk Heron, *1995, 42" x 52". To her hand-painted silk herons, Joan added neutrals that enhance, not overpower, the delicate gray-green. Bits of magenta, which bled from the ink, provided a subtle color cue, repeated here and there.*

happen by chance if the fabric piles are very broad and in my peripheral vision.

I love strange effects in nature. Who hasn't seen the green necks of a mallard duck or two in the local pond? I just saw about five hundred, swimming together, close. I can't get that image of iridescent green out of my head. Or the flashing movement of a flight of sandpipers—now brown, now silver! A scene that is common becomes something special when you are really looking. Riding one day, I was struck by a color combination that called for an assortment of clear fresh greens, without any blue sky. This didn't seem remarkable. Yet I filed the little list of colors—quite exquisite and detailed it was—and it seemed subtle, unusual, and just right at the time. One of these days.... Perhaps it will work for the mallards.

Joan Colvin lives in Bow, Washington.

Sally A. Sellers

The Color Dialogue

My response to color is immediate and visceral. Milliseconds after the initial encounter, I register shape, value, texture, and composition, but it is the color that first assaults my senses. It is color that is direct-wired to my emotions; it is color that charges my response before I even realize a response has occurred. There is so much to learn about color, and what an enchanting journey it is. I liken it to being on page 50 of a 800-page novel that I dearly love. I can easily measure the pleasure that lies ahead.

Color knowledge comes erratically, however, and just when I think I have achieved some small mastery, I discover how little I really understand. I believe that I have made friends with blue, only to be astounded by the way a certain turquoise changes when placed next to a particular orange. I replace one red with another that is a little more purple, and whammo!—a

good quilt becomes great. Color is relative, and the smallest shift in value or hue can dramatically alter a design. It is this dialogue between colors that intrigues me. They have so much to say.

I have strong opinions about color and the design process. I firmly believe that you must design with fabric, not colored pencils, markers, or a computer. The nuances that make or break a quilt cannot be duplicated using anything but the actual materials. Other tools may suggest the outcome, but they never tell the final color story.

Quilters should have lots of fabric. All greens are not the same. How will you know if a fabric has just enough yellow until you put up the swatch that has too much? And the one that has too little? Van Gogh might have known color in advance, but I don't, and I require a large, diverse pool of fabrics from which to choose.

It is the relationship between colors that matters, not the colors as they exist in isolation. "Ugly" colors can be gems. Sitting alone, they make me grimace, and I can't imagine why anyone would create that color, let alone use it. Then the same old miracle happens: you put a nauseating hue next to some sticky-sweet one, and suddenly they all sing. You don't need a lot of ugly, just enough to bring out the beauty of the surrounding colors.

Use your design wall and your intuition to discover what works and what doesn't. Be brutal in your critique. The fabric you thought was perfect may not be so great after all. Honor it by changing what surrounds it, or save it for the next quilt. Don't force it.

Take the time you need to develop a design, and never rush to sew. Restraint is difficult for people who love to stitch. Many

When You Are Very Still, *1996, 79" x 48". "When the inner voices of insecurity, guilt, and despair begin their chorus, I stop and gather myself. If I remain very still and simply breathe, peace returns." Analogous hues and neutrals carry out the quiet theme. Cottons and metallics are appliquéd on painted canvas.*

Ordinary Joy, *1996, 23" x 32".
"After several bleak years, I
promised myself I would never
again overlook the joy of an
ordinary day. This quilt
symbolizes the happiness to be
found in embracing simple
pleasures." Colorful squares
look even more intense against a
backdrop of blacks and
metallics; zipper pulls and
buttons embellish the surface.
The fabrics are commercial
cottons and synthetics.*

of us have such small windows of time
in which to do our work that we are
anxious to see something—anything—
emerge quickly. It's hard to look back on
a week's effort and realize that your
primary activity was auditioning colors
and shapes.

Try to think of time as an invest-
ment in your quilts. You may begin
with a dozen swatches pinned to your
design wall and end up days later with
a different dozen swatches—and sixty
reject swatches littering the tables and
floor. But now you've got the right

swatches, and it was clearly time well
spent. Time not well spent is time used
to sew a quilt that ultimately disappoints
you. Let your design ripen fully before
you begin.

*Sally Sellers lives in Vancouver,
Washington.*

Patty Hawkins

Colors Stratified

I am most fortunate to be this insane about color, and I am madly in love with the process that marries color and form. How color interacts when neighbored, how value suggests depth among shapes, how light dances across an abstract surface—these visual intrigues motivate my work.

I grew up in the South of the 1950s, a stultifying place and era for anyone interested in art. My mother was an accomplished seamstress, and she taught me the intricacies of sewing and the value of color. I can hear her saying, "People think green and blue don't work well together." But she worked them together anyway.

Fifteen years of painting with watercolors taught me about color and form, but my life in art changed in the mid 1980s when I saw an exhibit at the Denver Art Museum entitled *Craft: Poetry of the Physical*. Quilts by Nancy Crow, Michael James, Pam Studstill, and Risë Nagin ignited my imagination and fueled my desire to express ideas and images in quilts.

The Western landscape, with its ever-changing display of colors and shapes, has opened my eyes to the beauty of vast spaces. Paradoxically, this expansive environment requires that I use color sparingly. While showing slides to a group of quilters several years ago, I stopped abruptly at a projected image of the Mesa Verde cliff dwellings. The proverbial light went on: here, among a narrow range of natural colors and essential forms, was a wealth of inspiration. "Anasazi Dwellings: Colors Stratified" (1994) was my first attempt to reveal the infinite values in a limited number of hues. "Fluctuations: Colors Stratified #2" followed soon after.

The interplay of light, color, and pattern in the paintings of Monet, Cézanne, and Van Gogh also inspires my work. In particular, I am captivated by Monet's brushwork and his depiction of light and color through an awesome range of tints and hues. With hand-dyed fabric, rather than paint, I work to create gemlike areas glimpsed through an otherwise determined color field. These color jewels imply dimension and luminosity and add to the mystique of the color story.

I strive to sophisticate and enhance the visual interest in my quilts through the repetition of simple, exaggerated T and L shapes. I deliberately limit myself to a few

Fluctuations: Colors Stratified #2, *1995, 87" x 55". "The play of color and light in the Colorado summer skies inspired me to work with light and dark values in a narrow color range. I am infatuated with the complexities of color and value, which intimate the brush strokes of paintings."*

Abiquiu Abstracted, *1995, 33" x 52". Rocky tans, tree greens, and flower reds evoke the rich landscape of New Mexico. Neighboring colors in an abstracted field compliment and intensify each other.*

colors, but I use many values and intensities of these colors. A minimal palette pleases and challenges me aesthetically, and it is mesmerizing to design with simple shapes.

I dye-paint most of the fabrics in my quilts. Hand-dyed fabrics possess nuances and overlays of color that suggest the hues, textures, and patterns inherent in landscapes. I enjoy the change of pace that dyeing offers: dyeing produces an immediate, spontaneous result, while quilting is slow and exacting.

I work freehand, without preconceived or regulated shapes, cutting and sewing to the color that is speaking. The work in progress tells me which piece of fabric to place next, or which piece to remove. I have even stopped to dye fabric, to satisfy the need for more value contrast. It is this deliberate neighboring of low-key color and varied values that makes a quilt sing. The words of Cézanne motivate me to continue to play with tonal values: "Shadow is a color as light is, but less brilliant; light and shadow are only the relation of two tones. There is no such thing as line or modeling, there are only contrasts. These are not contrasts of light and dark, but the contrasts given by the sensation of color."

I feel strongly that quiltmakers share a responsibility to encourage others to enjoy the visual pleasures of contemporary art quilts. Art is powerful, coaxing the viewer to see life with a new eye and demanding a more thoughtful response. With my landscapes, I strive to synthesize nature's colors and forms and to encourage a positive and responsible outlook toward our environment.

Patty Hawkins lives in Lyons, Colorado.

Good Morning Sunshine *by Shirley Abruzzini, 1995, Gilroy, California, 66" x 80".*
A classic combination of blue and yellow balances cool and warm visual temperatures and suggests the sunlit skies of summer. The seemingly random placement of background values—some light, some dark—lends spontaneity to the design.

Feathered Star *by Tece Markel, Newcastle, California, 1996, 43½" x 43½". In this variation of a traditional favorite, analogous reds, oranges, golds, and mustardy browns are cooled by blue, the direct complement of orange. A mix of lights, darks, and brights keeps the eye moving.*

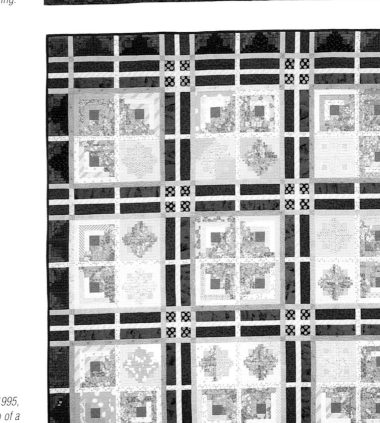

Lavish MacTavish *by Allison Lockwood, 1995, Shell Beach, California, 76" x 86". A photo of a tartan inspired Allison to make this plaidlike Log Cabin quilt. A Japanese-style floral with pinks, oranges, blues, and yellows was the color catalyst. Yellow-orange in the upper center blocks complements the dominant blues.*

Nature's Splendor *by Ellen Heck, 1995, Somis, California, 76" x 76". Nature's forms and colors are Ellen's inspiration. In this spectacular appliqué quilt, a polychromatic palette provides a full range of natural hues. To capture the coloration of fading flowers, Ellen used an assortment of hand-dyed fabrics.*

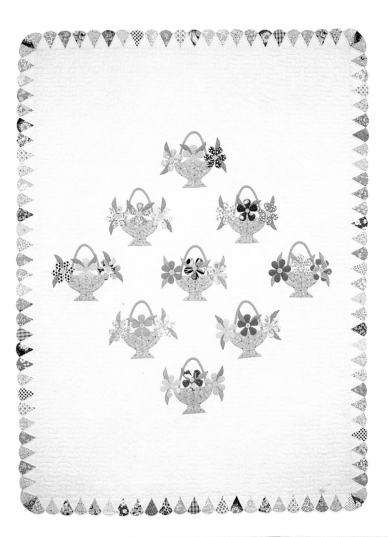

Baskets by Evelyn Sage, completed 1993, Meadow Vista, California, 75" x 98". Antique baskets in a variety of colors and stylized prints look fresh on a backdrop of white. Evelyn discovered this quilt as an unfinished top at a local antique shop. She quilted a multitude of baskets (which had been marked for appliqué), then added classic filler designs. Scraps from "Jewel Box" (page 64) became an ice-cream-cone border.

Baltimore Memories by Nadine Thompson, 1994, Pleasanton, California, 96" x 96". A traditional cream background showcases a wealth of colors and designs in this exquisite rendition of a Baltimore Album quilt. Most of the blocks are traditional; the center block and border are Nadine's designs.

Life's Harvest *by Lisa Ann Carrillo, 1995, Woodland Hills, California, 80" x 80". (From the collection of Ngaire Ullrich.) Lisa's love of nature shows in this vibrant quilt, a wedding gift for her niece. She began with the warm colors of autumn, balancing them with accents of cool blue, violet, turquoise, navy blue, and black. Plaids and small-scale prints lend vitality to the symbols of life.*

Dandelion Wine by Karen Burns, 1996, Granite Bay, California, 51" x 38". To frame an antique block, Karen chose reproduction fabrics in a variety of low-intensity hues. Light background prints add subtle texture and maintain the old-fashioned look. Topiary borders echo the center block and introduce pleasing curves to the design.

Firestorm by Gigi Phillips, 1995, Penn Valley, California, 46" x 46". Gigi took her inspiration for this off-center Pineapple quilt from a flame print, then carried out the color theme with analogous yellow, gold, orange, red-orange, and red. Neutral prints in gray, white, and charcoal black define the design and provide visual relief.

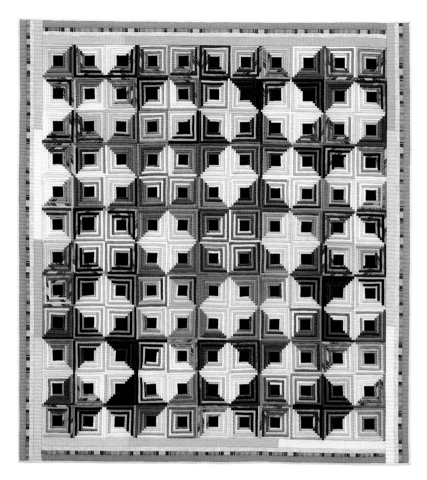

Tribute to a Kentucky Quilter *by Fran McEachern, 1995, Castro Valley, California, 46" x 50". A silk Log Cabin quilt made by Martha Tribble Hieatt in 1875 inspired Fran to stitch a miniature version in cotton fabrics. To capture the shading of silk, Fran used a variety of closely related colors in each block.*

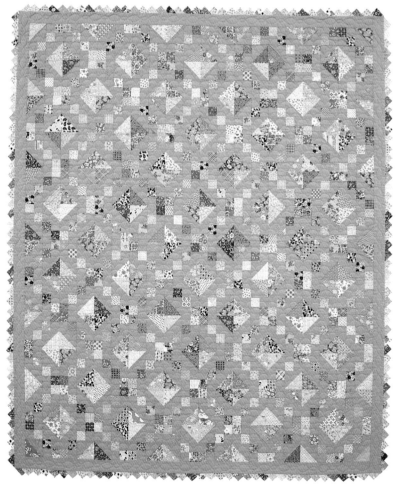

Jewel Box *by Evelyn Sage, 1992, Meadow Vista, California, 66" x 76½". Evelyn dipped into her collection of antique scraps to make this polychromatic version of an old-fashioned favorite. The Depression green background fabric, chosen for its scrappy look, is new. Prairie Points finish the edges with more jewels of color.*

Crazy for Chloe by Corinne Appleton, 1993, Jacksonville, Florida, 59" x 59". Value is the tie that binds a variety of gentle hues in this Crazy-quilt tribute to Chloe, Corinne's beloved cat. To differentiate the pieces, Corinne embroidered the seams in black. A green border with a complementary pink swag frames the blocks; silk ribbon flowers are in keeping with the soft scheme.

Irish Chain by Evelyn Sage, completed 1995, Meadow Vista, California, 54" x 54". Butterscotch yellow unites the borders and multicolored blocks in this sweet, simple quilt. The 1930s blocks were found in a box in a barn, along with just enough yellow fabric to complete the quilt.

A Feathered Star for Himself *by Eleanor Meaney, 1995, South Yarmouth, Massachusetts, 88" x 88".*
Eleanor combined complementary red and green with a neutral tan in her spectacular, award-winning
quilt. Mottled green-and-gold triangles frame the stars and contribute depth to the design. Elaborate
trapunto quilting adds actual and visual texture.

Due North, Gone South by Wendy Chizuko Simard, 1995, Colleyville, Texas, 80" x 106". Wendy began this quilt while in Canada and finished it in Texas, after 423 hours of quilting, which explains the title. Low-intensity navy blue, burgundy, and beige fabrics make up five different compass designs. The border geese "fly" north.

Crimson and Clover by Ruth Cattles Cottrell, 1995, Irving, Texas, 71" x 91". Complementary reds and greens predominate in this lively interpretation of an antique quilt. Ruth captured the mood with reproduction solids and new prints that look old. The borders consist of orange leaves cut from hand-dyed fabric and appliquéd to a batik; red rickrack adds the finishing touch.

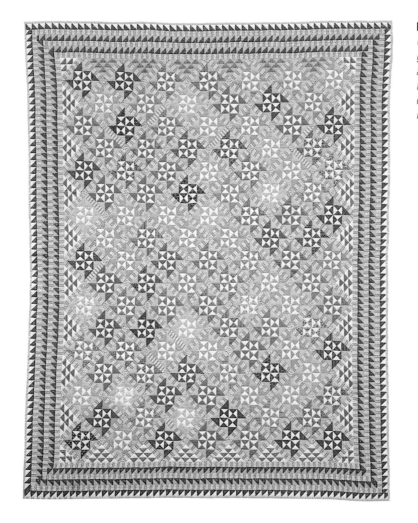

Big Dipper *by Maggie Potter, 1996, Walnut Creek, California, 60" x 74". Low-intensity greens, blues, grays, and even lavenders dance across the surface of this exuberant quilt. To tame the multi-colored scheme, Maggie limited each block to one fabric, plus a light and a neutral. Striped sashing unifies the design.*

Pixilated Plaids *by Lois Monieson, 1995, Kingston, Ontario, Canada, 60" x 63". Plaids cut off-grain twinkle in the company of deep, dark solids in this off-center Log Cabin quilt. The juxtaposition of intense and low-intensity color contributes to the luminous effect.*

Tennessee Waltz *by Phyllis Day, 1994, Citrus Heights, California, 84" x 100". (From the collection of Jeanne Jacobs.) Variety in color, value, and pattern lends depth and sophistication to this monochromatic scheme. Phyllis used many versions of violet, including magenta (red-violet), for the stars, and bits of other colors where she thought it needed splash.*

Canterbury Gardens *by Jaynette Huff, 1995, Conway, Arkansas, 96" x 96". Low-intensity colors in light, medium, and dark values establish a romantic mood in this original design. Jaynette began with a multicolored lead fabric and added harmonious prints in related hues. Fuchsia accents spark the quiet scheme.*

Freehand 6: Settling In *by Liz Axford, 1992, Houston, Texas, 60" x 62". Liz began this design with approximately twenty hand-dyed greens, from yellow-green through blue-green, in a range of values. To this analogous scheme she added complementary reds that go from clear scarlet to pink and rusty brown. Neutral solids set off the brights; black-and-white prints heighten the contrast.*

Purple Flower Woman *by Katy Widger, 1992, Edgewood, New Mexico, 55" x 55". Light and color flow from side to side and up and down in this polychromatic quilt. Memories of spring wildflowers and the hues in an Indian pot provided the color inspiration. Katy hand-dyed, printed, and painted the fabrics.*

Alpenglow *by Patty Hawkins, 1996, Lyons, Colorado, 51" x 47". "Alpenglow" is the reddish glow seen near the summit of mountains at sunrise or sunset. Using her hand dye-painted fabrics, Patty juxtaposed light and dark values in a narrow range of near-complementary reds and blues.*

Royal Palms of Paia *by Virginia Gaz, 1995, Cincinnati, Ohio, 31" x 47". To capture the complex colors and strong forms of Royal Palms, Virginia used a nearly triadic scheme of blue-green, red-violet, and yellow. Contrasting values and a wealth of patterns add to the mystique.*

Tessa, Cole, and a Man Have Tea *by Joan Basore, 1995, San Anselmo, California, 33" x 41". Delicious versions of yellow and violet (direct complements) combine in this fanciful quilt, made by Joan to celebrate her three grandchildren. Bits of every other color on the color wheel complete the palette. Most of the fabrics are hand dyed.*

Penelope's Art: A Tribute to My Mother's Cinnamon Rolls *by Laura Wasilowski, 1995, Elgin, Illinois, 46" x 45". Fond memories of her mother's baking inspired Laura's whimsical story quilt. A Formica-yellow tabletop accentuates complementary blues and oranges. Laura painted, silk-screened, and hand dyed the fabrics; the cinnamon swirls are stitched with hand-dyed perle cotton.*

Aquarium Life by Susan Webb Lee, 1990, Weddington, North Carolina, 45" x 74". This quilt displays symmetrical balance, in which one-half of the composition mirrors the other. To depict the workings of an aquarium, Susan chose intense colors and a variety of stylized and geometric prints.

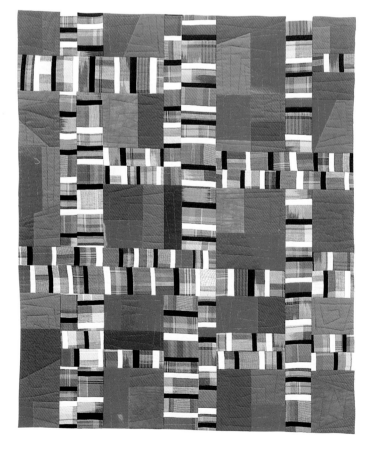

Grid Study #3: City Blocks by Michele Vernon, 1995, Falls Church, Virginia, 38" x 46". Think of this quilt as a map: the plaid bands represent busy city streets; in between are blocks and buildings. For the pieced background, Michele chose a far-ranging analogous scheme, from red-orange through blue-violet.

Persephone's Plight *by Virginia Gaz, 1993, Cincinnati, Ohio, 67" x 59". The intriguing pomegranate gave Virginia the opportunity to work with her favorite color, red. She used a wide variety of values, from pale tints to grayed tones and speckled shades, to portray the ruby seeds.*

The Aurora *by Patty Hawkins, 1996, Lyons, Colorado, 66" in diameter. Skewed Log Cabin blocks in the round take full advantage of the delicious nuances of hand-dyed fabrics. Stark contrasts in color and value suggest the third dimension. Light and dark rays advance, capturing the viewer's attention and inviting closer scrutiny. The fabrics were hand dyed by Patty.*

Kaleidoscopic XIII: Random Acts of Color
by Paula Nadelstern, 1994, Bronx, New York, 60" x 56". Paula captures the exquisite collision of free-falling color that occurs in a kaleidoscope. Intense colors look even more brilliant among low-intensity hues. Fluid color in the background and the border suggests the evanescence of kaleidoscopic color. In the instant a scope is handed from one to another, the colors maneuver into something new.

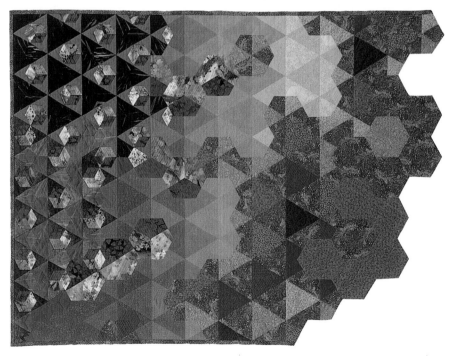

AutoFiction: Building Blocks *by Wendy Hill, 1995, Sunriver, Oregon, 65½" x 48½". Traditional Flower Garden hexagons in low-intensity hues metamorphose into luminous Building Blocks. Hand-dyed yellow and violet fabrics echo the transformation; the complementary colors merge in the "mutation zone."*

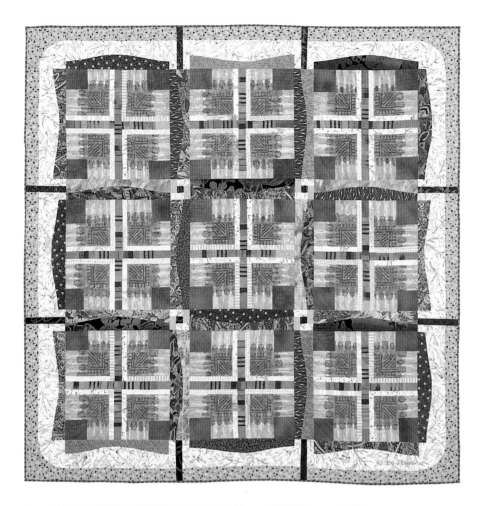

African Crosses by Elaine Plogman, 1996, Cincinnati, Ohio, 63" x 63". An African tie-dye fabric in low-intensity rose and green was the color catalyst for this sophisticated design. Near-neutrals in a mix of patterns and textures are the perfect color companions; strips of bright color accentuate the setting.

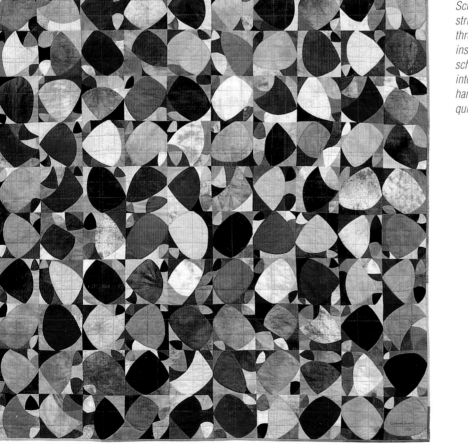

Near the Bridge at Winneboujou by Connie Scheele, 1995, Houston, Texas, 59" x 59". The striking impression of rocks and pebbles viewed through the clear water of a Wisconsin river inspired this improvisational quilt. Although the scheme at first reads as neutral, it includes low-intensity versions of many hues. The fabrics were hand dyed by Connie and Liz Axford. Hand quilted by Hallye Bone.

Memory Garden *by Jane Sassaman, 1995, Chicago, Illinois, 25½" x 37". Vintage florals and more recent black-and-white prints mingle in this graphic quilt. Blue accents electrify complementary reds and greens. Satin stitching on the leaves and thorns creates light and shadow, modulating color and adding actual texture.*

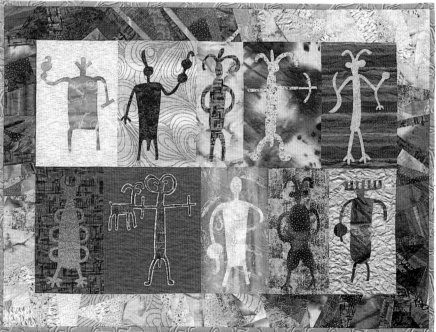

Coso Characters *by Charlotte Patera, 1995, Grass Valley, California, 42" x 31". Charlotte selected a variety of rock-like, earth-brown prints for her portrayal of the petroglyphs found in the Coso Range of southeastern California. Value, pattern, and texture play key roles in the monochromatic scheme. The figures are worked in positive and negative appliqué.*

Fourpatch I: June Backyard *by Sue Benner, 1993, Dallas, Texas, 86" x 105". Based on the Amish pattern known as Cross in the Square, this luminous quilt is Sue's interpretation of summer seen through her studio windows. Greens, reds, hot pinks, and oranges portray foliage and flower hues. Variations in value capture the effect of sunlight filtering through a canopy of trees. Sue hand dyed and hand painted many of the fabrics.*

Kelp Forest *by Ann Johnston, 1994, Lake Oswego, Oregon, 42" x 49". A let's-try-it-and-see experiment with curved piecing and hand-dyed fabrics led Ann to create the blocks for this oceany quilt. Analogous and near-complementary colors set up a pleasing visual tension. Random hand quilting in variegated rayon thread maintains the underwater theme.*

Emergence *by Melody Johnson, 1991, Cary, Illinois, 54" x 54". A lesson in color mixing, this quilt shimmers with pure and blended hues. Yellow and blue mingle to make green; blue and red merge into violet; red and yellow link through orange. To heighten the effect of connecting color, Melody strip-pieced 6½" blocks, cut each one into four squares, and then rotated the squares before repiecing.*

The Greenhouse Effect by Sally A. Sellers, 1994, Vancouver, Washington, 46" x 69". (From the collection of Dieter Hohnke.) Near-complements of red-violet and green, and blue-green and orange establish a pleasing color cadence. In Sally's vision, the individual house unit reverberates in the larger image, just as individual choices determine society's stance.

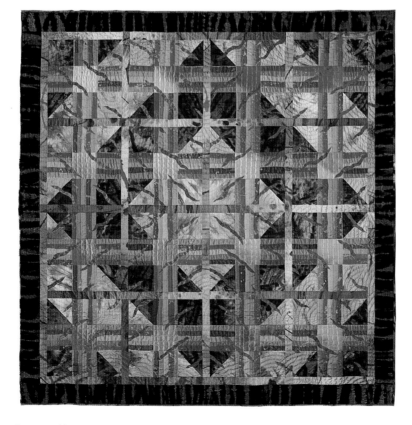

Hair Raising by Sue Benner, 1992, Dallas, Texas, 73" x 73". Sue enjoys combining unlikely colors in ways that make them look as though they were made for each other. The chartreuse-to-pink squares, cut from one piece of hand-dyed fabric, maintain their order across the quilt, lending continuity to the design. The orange squiggles, in complementary contrast to the blue, jar the surface with unexpected color.

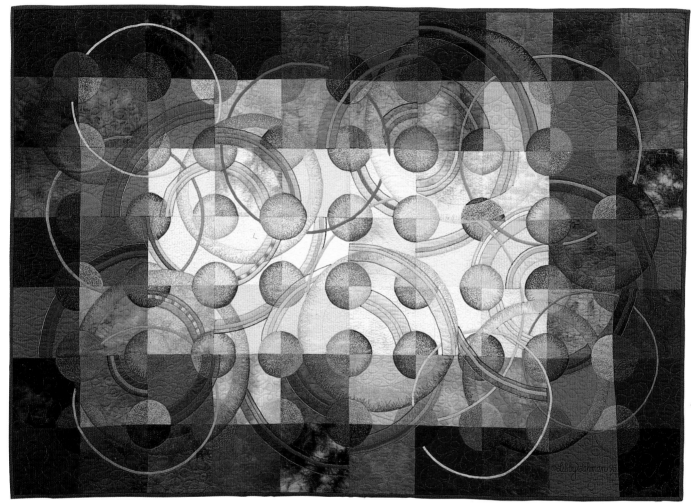

Rim Shots *by Libby Lehman, 1995, Houston, Texas, 59" x 41". (From the collection of Donna Moog Nussbaum.) A study in color and composition, this quilt displays the elements and principles of good design. Net overlays and dense stitching add texture to a base of pieced circles and squares. The juxtaposition and layering of shapes creates the illusion of depth; luminosity comes from a sophisticated blend of hues, values, and intensities.*

a color workshop

Now it's your turn to put the color concepts and principles to work using your favorite fabrics. On the next ten pages, you'll find nine exercises that explore various aspects of color. You'll have the most fun if you do these exercises with a group of friends, or in a workshop setting, such as a class or a guild get-together. But don't hesitate to do them on your own. There's nothing like hands-on experience to teach you about color—and perhaps inspire the color scheme for your next quilt.

The cutting instructions given in each exercise are for mock blocks. See page 37 for tips on making mock blocks.

Value

To recap the concept of value:

- Value is the lightness or darkness of a color.
- Contrasts in value create depth in a block or a quilt.
- Value is relative: Whether a medium-value color looks light or dark depends on the surrounding values.
- Value determines the design in a block or a quilt.

The following coloring exercise illustrates the role of value in determining a design and establishing depth. It also demonstrates, to a lesser extent, the relativity of value.

To do this exercise:

1. Make 3 photocopies of the blank setting of the Sky Rocket blocks shown below.
2. Gather 3 pencils, one light, one medium, and one dark in value. You can color the blocks with a No. 2 writing pencil, varying the pressure to create three distinct values, or with three gray pencils. If you choose to work with colored pencils, use colors that form a classic color combination, such as triadic red-orange, blue-violet, and yellow-green, or any three pleasing hues. Use the color that is naturally lightest for the light value and the colors that are naturally medium and dark for the other two values.
3. For Set #1, copy the values shown in the example, the traditional value placement for Sky Rocket. In this set, the light- and medium-value ninepatch units appear to float above kaleidoscope units formed by the dark-value points.
4. For Set #2, follow the value placement indicated. In this arrangement, the ninepatch units float high above the points, and the dark-value squares form strong diagonal chains.
5. In Set #3, follow the value placement indicated. A transparency effect occurs, and the blocks appear to bloom as three-dimensional units.

The relative values and colors may appear to vary slightly in each set, the result of differences in their placement. In Set #2, for example, the juxtaposition of the light and dark values accentuates the contrast, while in Set #3, the values flow from dark to light, diminishing the differences.

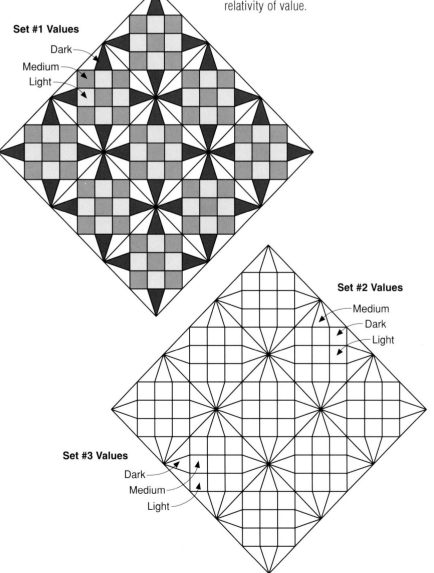

Set #1 Values
Dark
Medium
Light

Set #2 Values
Medium
Dark
Light

Set #3 Values
Dark
Medium
Light

Visual Temperature

A simple Double Four Patch is an ideal block for experimenting with color and visual temperature.

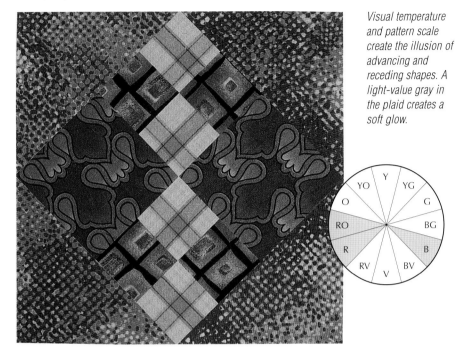

Visual temperature and pattern scale create the illusion of advancing and receding shapes. A light-value gray in the plaid creates a soft glow.

To recap the concept of visual temperature:

- Warm colors tend to advance while cool colors recede.
- Value can accentuate the illusion of depth created by different visual temperatures. Light, warm colors appear to be farthest from dark, cool colors.
- Intensity can maximize differences in visual temperature. Intense warm colors advance dramatically when placed next to low-intensity cool colors.

In the Double Four Patch block shown above, the warm, light-value plaid and the intense red print advance. (Using warm colors for the small shapes enhances the effect because the eye reads smaller shapes as being closer.) Similar design lines unite the red and red-orange fabrics, strengthening the illusion that the small squares float above the background.

The cool blue prints, which are darker in value and less intense, recede. Bits of red-orange in the blue background echo the warm colors in the small squares.

To do this exercise:

1. Choose 2 warm colors, one light in value and one medium, for the small squares. If possible, choose fabrics with related patterns in similar scales.
2. Choose 2 cool colors, one medium in value and one dark, for the large squares and background triangles. If possible, choose a medium- or large-scale pattern for the large squares.

   The warm and cool colors don't need to be exact complements; here they are near-complements of blue, red, and red-orange. You can achieve a similar effect with any two colors, one warm, the other cool.
3. Make the mock block according to the cutting instructions, following the temperature and value placement shown in the example.

Cutting Instructions
9" Double Four Patch mock block:

From each of 2 warm colors, cut:
4 squares, each 1⅝", for the small squares

From a dark-value cool color, cut:
2 squares, each 3³⁄₁₆", for the large squares

From a medium-value cool color, cut:
2 squares, each 4½". Cut the squares once diagonally to make 4 half-square triangles.

Just for Fun ...

To experiment with temperature relativity (page 8), pull a red-violet fabric from your stash. Pull all of your true violets and arrange them in a fan, then pull your true reds and fan them. Cut two small squares of the red-violet fabric and place one square on each fabric fan. Notice that the red-violet looks warm against the violets, which are cooler in comparison, but cool against the warmer reds.

Intensity

Variable Star is an excellent block for experimenting with intensity because the design is simple, with a definite foreground and background. This exercise also involves the dimensions of color and value.

To recap the concept of intensity:

- Intense colors are pure and bright; low-intensity colors are grayed and dull.
- Intensity is about color purity; value is about the lightness or darkness of color.

Patterns and solids combine easily when the colors are low in intensity. This scheme is a tetrad (page 19) of red-orange and blue-green, and violet and yellow. (The yellow is very light in value and low in intensity.)

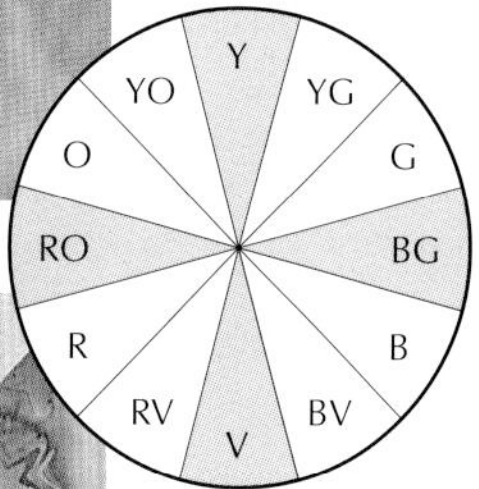

- Intense colors often advance, and low-intensity colors often recede, although size and composition play equally important roles in establishing depth.

To do this exercise:

1. If you're working from your stash, pull a variety of fabrics with low-intensity color and separate them according to value (light, medium, and dark). If you can create a classic color combination, such as the tetrad of sea green (blue-green), salmon (red-orange), grape (violet), and wheat (pale yellow) shown here, that's great, but it's not necessary. Any harmonious, low-intensity colors in a range of values will work.

2. If you're buying new fabric, it's easiest to begin with a low-intensity lead fabric, and then add other low-intensity fabrics, just as you would in building a cast of fabrics. Strive for variety in value, pattern style, and pattern scale.

3. Make the mock block according to the cutting instructions, following the value placement shown in the example.

Cutting instructions
9" Variable Star mock block:

From a medium-value fabric, cut:
1 square, 3", for the center square

From a second medium-value fabric, cut:
1 square, 3". Cut the square twice diagonally to make 4 quarter-square triangles to surround the center square.

From a dark-value fabric, cut:
2 squares, each 3". Cut the squares twice diagonally to make 8 quarter-square triangles for the star points.

From a light-value fabric, cut:
5 squares, each 3". Cut 1 square twice diagonally to make 4 quarter-square triangles for the background.

Just for Fun ...

Add a lighter-value, low-intensity fabric to your cast and make a series of four Balkan Puzzle mock blocks (at left). The large triangles are quarter-square triangles cut from 4½" squares, the small triangles are half-square triangles cut from 2¼" squares, and the center square is 3¼".

A light-value, pink-beige background fabric alters the value relationships between the fabrics and spaces out the low-intensity color.

Pattern and Texture

This exercise emphasizes pattern and texture, again using a Variable Star block.

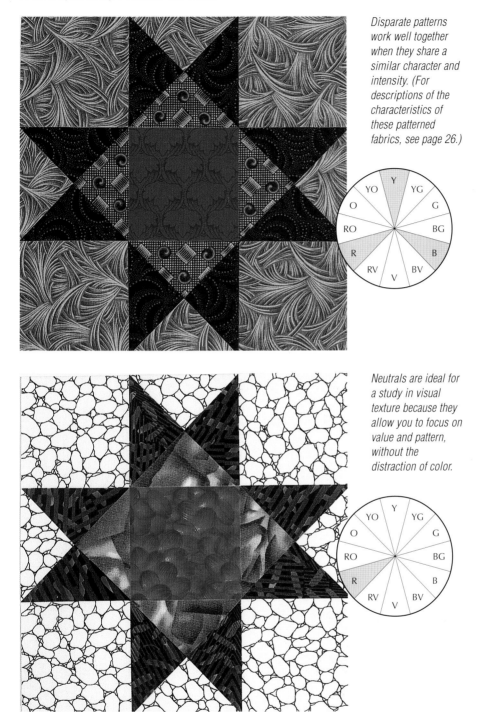

Disparate patterns work well together when they share a similar character and intensity. (For descriptions of the characteristics of these patterned fabrics, see page 26.)

Neutrals are ideal for a study in visual texture because they allow you to focus on value and pattern, without the distraction of color.

To recap the concept of pattern and texture:

- Patterns and textures have certain characteristics, such as ground color, density, and scale, that determine their character.
- Patterns and textures come in a variety of styles, from representational to painterly.
- Variety plus unity equals harmony in pattern combinations. For a traditional effect, vary the pattern scale and style while striving for unity in pattern character. In the first star, all the patterns have a traditional character.

You can vary the pattern character of the fabrics in a quilt and still achieve harmony, as long as there is unity in other aspects of the design, such as color. In "Tipsy Tiles" (page 118), the fabrics vary widely in pattern character but maintain the triadic scheme.

To do this exercise:

1. Whether you're working from your stash or buying new fabric, choose a lead fabric, preferably one with two or more colors. In the first star, the small-scale, medium-density fabric surrounding the center square is the lead fabric. Its colors form a triad of low-intensity primaries (red, yellow/gold, and blue).
2. Keying off your lead fabric, choose three more patterned fabrics that vary in style, scale, and density. For a traditional block, select fabrics of similar intensity and character but different values.
3. Make the mock block according to the instructions on the facing page and the value placement shown in the example.

Just for Fun ...

Make a block similar to the second star using nonrepresentational patterns that read as visual texture. Again, vary the scale and the value, but maintain a consistent character.

Color Combinations

Analogous red, red-orange, orange, and yellow-orange fabrics in light and dark values combine for a simple Log Cabin block. Complementary blue is the obvious choice for the center square.

A split complement of red-orange, blue, and green emphasizes the cool hues in this Chimneys and Cornerstones block.

To recap color combinations:

See pages 13–20 for detailed discussions of these color schemes, and refer to the color wheels on pages 10–11 for help in selecting colors.

- A neutral combination consists of black, white, and gray, plus light-value, low-intensity hues.
- A monochromatic scheme is limited to one color, such as blue-green, but includes a variety of values and intensities. Neutrals space out the color in monochromatic schemes.
- An analogous combination takes in three to five adjacent colors on the color wheel. For example, yellow-green, green, blue-green, and blue make up a four-color analogous scheme.
- A direct complement consists of any two colors opposite each other on the color wheel. Yellow-orange and blue-violet are direct complements; so are red and green, and blue and orange.

- A split complement contains one color and the two colors on each side of its complement, such as yellow, red-violet, and blue-violet.
- A double complement consists of two adjacent colors and their complements. Blue and orange, and blue-violet and yellow-orange make up a double complement.
- A double split complement splits a pair of direct complements to make a four-color combination. Complements blue-green and red-orange, for example, can be split into blue and orange, and red and green.
- A triad consists of three colors equidistant on the color wheel. Green, violet, and orange form a triad of secondaries.
- A tetrad is made up of four colors equidistant on the color wheel. Yellow-green, red-violet, blue, and orange form a tetrad.
- A polychromatic color combination includes colors from all around the color wheel, but not necessarily every color.

To do this exercise:

There's no better way to get acquainted with the classic color combinations than to practice using them in simple block designs. This exercise is especially well suited to a class or group setting, where quilters can pool their fabrics.

If you find the prospect of sharing your fabrics painful, consider what you have to gain. Swapping small amounts of fabric greatly increases your color options, and what you lose by sharing will be offset by the quantum leap you make in your understanding of color. You'll also have the chance to play with colors not in your stash, providing a great opportunity to broaden your color horizons. Best of all, you'll have more fun.

You can do these exercises in one of two formats, depending on the fabrics available to you. If you or your group has lots of fabric, consider making basic Log Cabin or Chimneys and Cornerstones mock blocks. Everyone likes these blocks and they're easy to make.

Contemporary prints with minimal color and dappled light lend an air of mystery to a neutral scheme.

In this Churn Dash block, the center square fabric displays a classic tetrad (page 19) of red and green, and yellow-orange and blue-violet.

If you have a limited stash, try your hand at the color combinations using a traditional Churn Dash block. It requires fewer fabrics, yet the design is complex enough to be interesting. It's especially suited to three- or four-color schemes.

All of the color combinations work in the basic Log Cabin, Chimneys and Cornerstones, and Churn Dash blocks. However, a split complement, triad, or three-color analogous combination is a bit easier to create in the Churn Dash block.

Cutting Instructions
7" Log Cabin or Chimneys and Cornerstones mock block:

Cut 1" squares
Cut 1"-wide strips

Cutting Instructions
9" Churn Dash mock block:

Cut 1 square, 3", for the center

Cut 2 squares, each 3". Cut the squares in half once crosswise to make 4 inner rectangles.

Cut 2 squares, each 3". Cut the squares once diagonally to make 4 half-square triangles.

Cut 4 squares, each 3". Cut 2 squares once diagonally to make 4 half-square triangles for the background. Cut the remaining 2 squares in half once crosswise to make 4 background rectangles.

Just for Fun ...

Make 9 of the 10 color combinations in the basic Log Cabin, Chimneys and Cornerstones, or Churn Dash block designs, then glue the mock blocks to a large sheet of paper for a mock color sampler. To achieve harmony amid the color diversity, use fabrics that are similar in character and intensity.

Other Log Cabin designs are wonderful formats for exploring color combinations: Off-set Log Cabin is ideal for a light/dark monochromatic scheme; Courthouse Steps is perfect for a double split complement; and Pineapple is well-suited to two- and four-color combinations.

Luminosity

Luminosity is easy to achieve with painterly prints, batiks, and hand-dyed fabrics.

This exercise is perfect for a class setting, where students can swap small amounts of key fabrics.

To recap the concept of luminosity:

- Lighter values glow when surrounded by darker values.
- More intense colors glow when surrounded by less intense colors.
- Luminosity is easiest to achieve when the glowing area is small in relation to the surrounding area.

To do this exercise, start with a group of fabrics that includes:

- Warm, light-value, intense hues for the glowing area
- Cool, dark-value, low-intensity hues for the background

Your colors may form a classic color combination, such as complementary orange and blue, or they may come from all around the color wheel. The essential ingredient is contrast in visual temperature, value, and intensity.

Cut 2" squares and arrange them on your design wall or on a piece of flannel, placing a few warm/light/bright squares near the center and surrounding them with cool/dark/dull squares. Try for an area of highlight, using your lightest/brightest square and smooth transitions from the glow to the darker areas.

Simultaneous Contrast

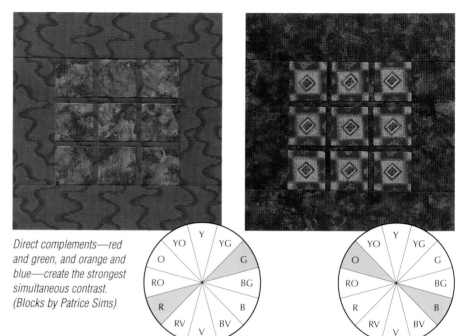

Direct complements—red and green, and orange and blue—create the strongest simultaneous contrast. (Blocks by Patrice Sims)

This is one special effect that you must do to appreciate.

To recap the concept of simultaneous contrast:

- Intense complementary colors appear to vibrate when placed side by side.
- The colors need not be direct complements; simultaneous contrast can occur with intense near-complements.
- Varying the values and lowering the intensity of the colors diminishes the effect of simultaneous contrast.

A simple format of small squares on a background square illustrates this powerful effect. Choose intense versions of two complements, such as orange and blue, or red and green. Cut nine 1½" squares of one of the fabrics and arrange them, with small spaces in between, on a 9" square of the complementary fabric. Step back and analyze the effect: if the hues are intense and similar in value, you will perceive an intensification of the colors, especially at the edges.

Just for Fun ...

Now try this exercise with intense analogous colors, such as orange and red. You'll discover that a square of intense orange will look relatively dull and lifeless when placed on a background of intense red, demonstrating that simultaneous contrast occurs with contrasting, not related, colors.

Transparency

A simple Nine Patch block is perfect for exploring transparency because the ends of the source colors show, leading the eye to the mixed color in the center square. Refer to "Back to Basics" on page 23 for a quilt that features transparency effects in Nine Patch blocks.

A Transparency of Value

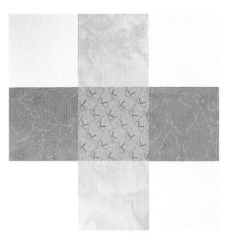

A value transparency mixes light, medium, and dark values.

For this transparency study, choose a light, dark, and medium value of the same color. If possible, use a medium-value color that is midway between the source colors in terms of value, such as the medium-value yellow-orange in the center of the block above. If you don't have three distinct values of the same color, work with light, medium, and dark values of different colors of the same intensity. (Keeping the intensities similar helps to fool the eye, even when the colors aren't correct.)

A Transparency of Value and Color

Any transparency is more convincing when design lines or patterns appear to continue from the source colors through the mixed color.

Once you understand a value transparency, bring color into the equation. Refer to the color wheels on pages 10–11, if necessary, for help in choosing the source colors and the mixed color. You can work with two primaries and a secondary, such as the blue, yellow, and blue/yellow and blue/yellow/green fabrics above. Or choose three analogous colors such as red, red-violet and violet. Avoid complementary colors; they combine to form a neutral gray. Make one source color light in value and the other dark; choose a medium-value version of the mixed color.

A Transparency of Color and Design

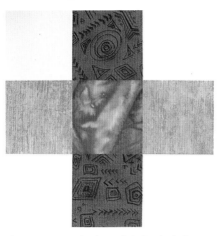

A transparency of color and design fools the eye into seeing a color mixture.

For this sophisticated transparency, choose a multi-colored fabric that has at least two distinct colors, then search for source fabrics with these colors. You can enhance the transparency effect by relating the multi-colored fabric to the source fabrics in terms of design as well as color. If, for example, your multi-colored fabric has a swirling pattern, choose source fabrics that echo or continue the swirls.

Cutting instructions
9" Nine Patch mock block:

Cut 3" squares, 2 for each source color and 1 for the mixed color

Nature's Colors

Nature provides the color cues for a triadic scheme.

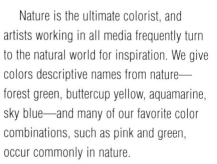

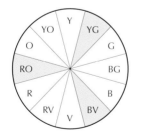

Nature is the ultimate colorist, and artists working in all media frequently turn to the natural world for inspiration. We give colors descriptive names from nature—forest green, buttercup yellow, aquamarine, sky blue—and many of our favorite color combinations, such as pink and green, occur commonly in nature.

The only skill you need to access color in nature is that of careful observation. Walk through a garden in full flower or peruse the pages of garden magazines and catalogs and you'll find a wealth of color ideas for quilts. Following are just a few of nature's color combinations.

Complementary color occurs widely in nature:

- A bi-color yellow and violet iris displays delicate tints.
- Red holly berries contrast colorfully with shiny green leaves.
- Blue-violet hydrangeas and yellow-orange lilies flower together in complementary harmony.

Monochromatic and analogous color combinations are just as prevalent in nature:

- Burgundy accentuates the edges of pale pink dianthus.
- Salmon lilies have brilliant yellow-orange throats.
- Sweet peas come in analogous hues, from pink through blue-violet.

Neutral colors are also well represented in nature, although they are often overlooked:

- Succulents display neutral and near-neutral hues.
- Birch bark colors go from chalky white to charcoal gray.

(Above) Alternating peach and pale yellow background fabrics creates a subtle transparency effect.

(Left) The star block known as Aunt Dinah calls for a full cast of fabrics in a variety of values and patterns.

You can draw inspiration from the colors in individual plants, such as purple pansies with yellow centers and green leaves. Or, let a group of different plants serve as the color catalyst. The photos on the facing page are an example of the second approach. Refer to the color wheel as you analyze these colors from nature:

Hydrangea blue, sometimes called lavender-blue or periwinkle, is a tint of blue-violet; coral is a tint of red-orange; peach is a tint of orange; and olive is a shade (dark value) of yellow-green. Now look again at your color wheel and you will see that three of these colors—blue-violet, red-orange, and yellow-green—form a triad of intermediate colors.

There is no lead fabric in the cast shown here, but the fabrics vary in value (light, medium, and dark) and pattern style (geometric, stylized, and near-solid). The colors are fairly intense, and the fabrics are contemporary in character.

- Coral squares surrounded by light-value periwinkle triangles and darker-value olive star points are logical choices. The contrasting values and colors keep the design lines crisp.
- The dark star points suggest light background pieces, either periwinkle or peach. Alternating a light peach near-solid with a pale yellow basket-weave print makes the stars appear to float. Reversing the placement of these fabrics from block to block creates a subtle transparency (page 23), as if the stars with the lightest background overlap the others.
- Darker-value periwinkle and coral fabrics in the corners form an on-point square and four-patch unit where the four blocks meet.

To do this exercise:

Using the color wheel and plants or photos as a guide, choose a combination of colors from nature. Gather a group of fabrics in the colors you have chosen and make 4 mock blocks according to the following instructions.

Cutting Instructions
9" Aunt Dinah mock block:

For the center square, cut 1 square, 3"

For the small triangles surrounding the center square, cut 1 square, 3". Cut the square twice diagonally to make 4 quarter-square triangles.

For the star points, cut 2 squares, each 3". Cut the squares twice diagonally to make 8 quarter-square triangles.

For the small triangles between the star points, cut 1 square, 3". Cut the square twice diagonally to make 4 quarter-square triangles.

For the large light triangles, cut 2 squares, each 3". Cut the squares once diagonally to make 4 half-square triangles.

For the corner squares, cut 4 squares, each 1½"

For the large dark corner triangles, cut as you did the light triangles. Glue a 1½" corner square to each dark triangle.

color studies

Diatoms and Wrinkled Whelk

by Joan Colvin

Color Study A

Color Study B

Diatoms and Wrinkled Whelk *by Joan Colvin, 1996, Bow, Washington, 34" x 34". Shell colors and shapes lend themselves to simple yet sophisticated color studies. Joan illustrates the possibilities with three designs. Romantic, bold, or realistic—the choice is yours.*

Color Study C

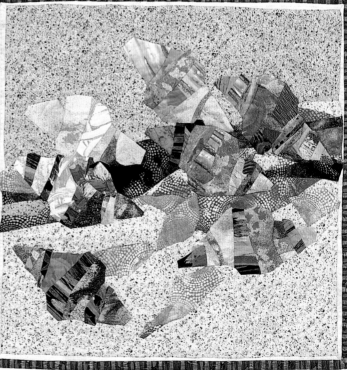

Finished Sizes: 34" x 34"
Skill Level: Intermediate

Color Cues

Using three different approaches to color and composition, Joan explores the exquisite hues and delicate forms of shells. Choose the technique that appeals to you. In making your choice, remember that technique influences the mood of a design, which in turn influences color choices. Shells suggest a variety of palettes and compositions.

- In Color Study A, sweet florals and stylized neutrals set a delicate, romantic mood. The strip-pieced shells are set in traditional diagonal rows.
- In Color Study B, contemporary stripes and stylized prints in vibrant hues bring energy and movement to the design. The strip-pieced shells are arranged and appliquéd in loosely diagonal rows.
- In Color Study C, neutral colors and natural textures capture the lines and shapes of shells. The shells are composed of curved pieces and appliquéd in a free-form composition.

The basic shell pattern is simple yet adaptable to many techniques and arrangements. Because the outer edges are pleasing, there is little chance of awkward forms developing. You can modify the interior of the shell in any way that suits your design. You can also vary the size of the finished piece and make as many shells as you like.

You have a similar freedom with color choices. Forget about what is appropriately "shell colored" and work with harmonious hues in a range of values, intensities, patterns, and textures. Decorator fabrics and contemporary quilting fabrics are ideal for these designs. Try one of the studies in a monochromatic scheme (page 14), with neutrals. Or, choose your colors as Joan does:

- Select a keynote, or lead, fabric; then add colors that enhance it. Avoid overwhelming your keynote fabric with too many or too varied supporting fabrics. Also beware of failing to deal with your keynote fabric; that is, not following its lead or not supporting it adequately with other fabrics.
- As you select your lead and supporting fabrics, think about the mood you wish to convey. Do you want your piece to be formal? Childlike? Realistic? Your lead fabric may express without doubt the mood you have chosen, but if it does not, you can establish mood through the use of color.
- Consider color, pattern, and texture simultaneously. It's difficult to separate color from pattern and texture. Visual texture, pattern density, motifs, and the regularity or irregularity of the design all influence the character of a fabric just as color does. A pink floral, for example, may be naturalistic and romantic or stylized and contemporary.

Unless you work with color only in pure form, all of the design elements come into play, perhaps creating confusion. On the bright side, the permutations and possibilities are without end.

Note: Yardage requirements for the background fabrics may vary depending on the design of the fabric and the way you piece the background. Before you buy your background fabrics, look at them carefully to determine how you want to piece them.

Color Study A

Of the three designs, this one is the most traditional in technique and composition. Classic florals, calicoes, and stripes in low-intensity peach and mauve, along with neutrals, make up the fabric palette.

The orderly composition and soft colors convey a gentle, romantic mood. A new geometric begins to take shape, and the shells fade in and out as they are lost in the greater pattern. That is the purpose of the straight piecing: the uncontoured shapes become part of the network of lines.

Materials: 44"-wide fabrics

Scraps of assorted pastel and neutral prints for shells
⅜ yd. dark-value neutral for background
Scraps of light- and dark-value neutrals for background
1 yd. (lengthwise strips) or ⅝ yd. (crosswise strips) fabric for border
1⅛ yds. fabric for backing
Batting

Cutting and Piecing

All measurements include ¼"-wide seam allowances.

1. From the assorted pastel and neutral prints, cut various-width strips and strip-piece a section large enough to accommodate the shell pattern shown on pages 98–99. Following the orientation shown below, cut out the shell, leaving a ¼"-wide seam allowance. Piece and cut the desired number of shells.

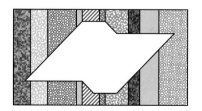

2. From the background fabrics, cut 1½"- and 2"-wide strips. Sew the 1½" strips to the angled edges of each shell, pivoting at the corners. Sew a 2" strip to the left edge of each shell.

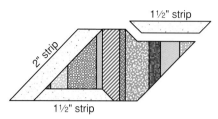

3. Join the shells into diagonal rows, adding pieces of background fabric as needed. Join the rows, offsetting the shells.

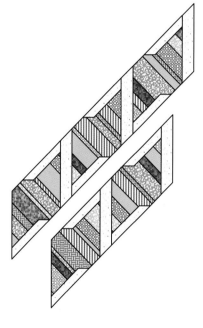

4. Add a mitered-corner border wide enough to wrap to the back.
5. Layer the quilt top with batting and backing; baste.
6. Quilt as desired.
7. Wrap the border to the back and blindstitch in place.

Color Study B

This variation also features randomly strip-pieced shells, but they are arranged irregularly and appliquéd to a pieced background. The composition is enigmatic, teasing the eye with shells that advance visually, but as extensions of the sea-floor pattern.

Bold prints and vibrant colors set a contemporary mood. The lead fabric, used for the background, demands stylized supporting fabrics in hues that hold their own.

When you work with a lead fabric, you spread the color as if you had painted the fabric, and you are continuing to paint with the same palette. You experience color explosively; you think "colored shells," but you take them all in at once. The effect is graphic and stylish, part fantasy yet grounded in natural lines.

Materials: 44"-wide fabric

Scraps of assorted prints for shells
¾ yd. lead fabric for pieced background
¾ yd. neutral fabric for pieced background
½ yd. lengthwise stripe for border
1⅛ yds. fabric for backing
⅜ yd. fabric for binding
Batting

Cutting and Piecing

All measurements include ¼"-wide seam allowances.

1. From the assorted prints, cut various-width strips and strip-piece a section large enough to accommodate the shell pattern on pages 98–99. Following the orientation shown below, cut out the shell, leaving a ¼"-wide seam allowance. Piece and cut the desired number of shells.

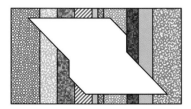

2. Piece the background fabrics as desired.
3. Appliqué the shells to the background.
4. Add a mitered-corner border.
5. Layer the quilt top with batting and backing; baste.
6. Quilt as desired.
7. Bind the edges.

Color Study C

This study illustrates how subtle changes in color and pattern can set a very different scene. Abstract prints and textures in subdued, near-neutral hues suggest realistic shells and the gentle fall of natural light. The eye is drawn to the color and form of each shell in turn, although you have to search a little for some. Here the background is barely noticeable, except as a design device that allows some shells to stand out while others merge with the sea floor.

The interior lines of the shells are curved, with random strip piecing in some segments. The outer edges are contoured and appliquéd randomly to the pieced background.

Materials: 44"-wide fabrics

Scraps of assorted prints and textures
    for shells
¾ yd. each of two background fabrics
1⅛ yds. fabric for backing
⅜ yd. fabric for binding
Batting

Cutting and Piecing

All measurements include ¼"-wide seam allowances.

1. Using the pattern on pages 98–99, make templates for the shell sections.
2. Cut and piece each shell, strip piecing some segments before cutting them out.
3. Piece the background fabrics as desired.
4. Appliqué the shells to the background, contouring the edges.

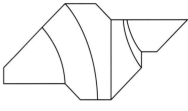

Pattern

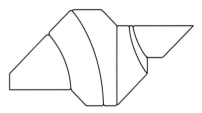

Contoured Shell

5. Layer the quilt top with batting and backing; baste.
6. Quilt as desired.
7. Bind the edges.

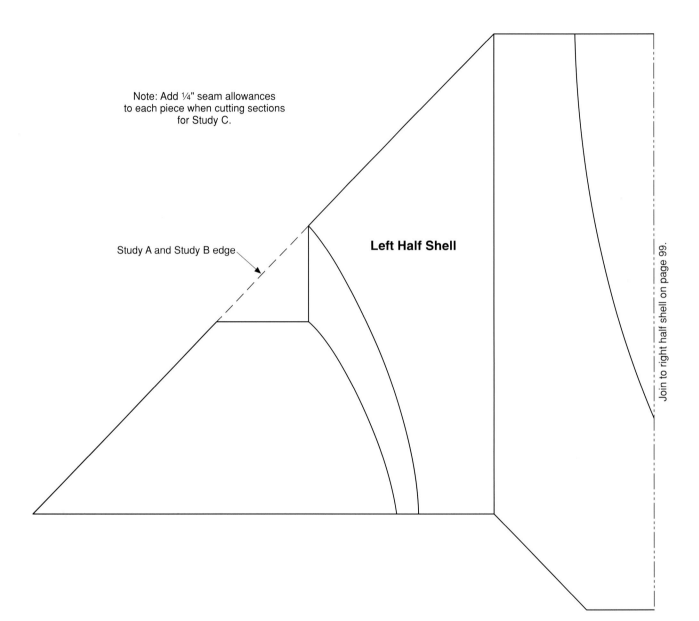

Note: Add ¼" seam allowances
to each piece when cutting sections
for Study C.

Study A and Study B edge

Left Half Shell

Join to right half shell on page 99.

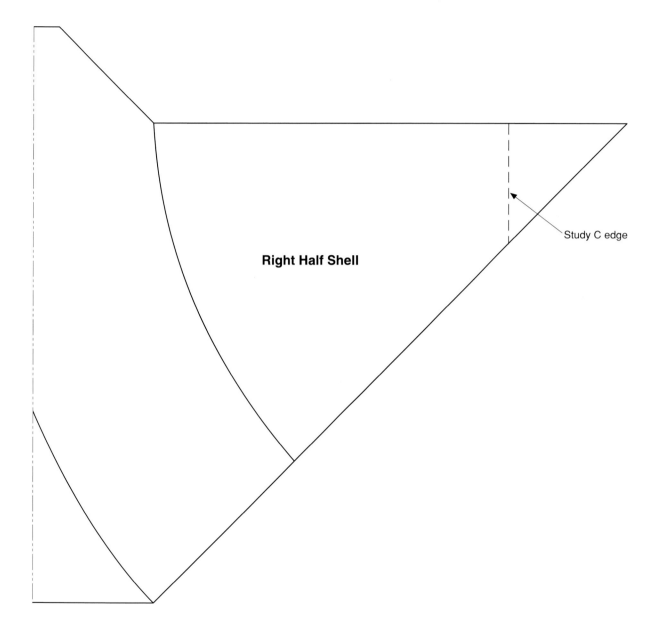

Right Half Shell

Study C edge

Gypsy Crossroads
by Susan M. Connoley

Color Cues

You can explore any of the direct complementary color combinations (page 16) using a traditional Monkey Wrench block and the simple setting you see here. Sue began with complementary yellow and violet, then expanded her scheme to include related colors and accents of intense green and blue-green.

Contrasting values and a lively mix of patterns give this quilt its light, airy look. The dark-value prints that make up the blocks advance visually, while the light-value background prints recede. The on-point blocks appear to float, thanks to side and corner setting triangles that are slightly darker in value than the background prints.

The paisley border is in keeping with the scale and character of the blocks. Although it's difficult to assign a color to this fabric, it works because it echoes colors, patterns, and textures found throughout the blocks.

If you wish to make this quilt in a different color combination, choose fabrics in the values indicated in the materials list.

Gypsy Crossroads by Susan M. Connoley, 1995, Gig Harbor, Washington, 48" x 57". Soft yellows glow in the company of violet and near-violet prints. A blend of patterns and textures brings vitality to this classic color combination.

Finished Size: 48" x 57"
Skill Level: Beginner

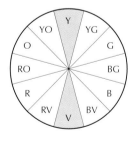

Materials: 44"-wide fabric

13 rectangles, each at least 5" x 10", of assorted yellow or cream (light value) prints for blocks

13 rectangles, each at least 5" x 10", of assorted violet (medium value) prints for blocks

¼ yd. total assorted scraps of yellow or cream (light value) prints for blocks

¼ yd. total assorted scraps of green and blue-green (medium value) prints for blocks and pieced strips

½ yd. total assorted scraps of violet (dark value) prints for block center squares and binding

½ yd. multi-colored violet (light value) print for setting triangles

⅜ yd. black (dark value) print for inner border*

1 yd. multi-colored (dark value) print for outer border

2⅞ yds. fabric for backing (crosswise seam)

Batting

Beads and rayon embroidery ribbon (optional)

*If you want to use a lengthwise stripe as Sue did, you will need 1⅛ yds.

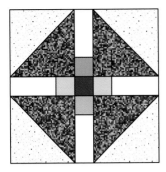

Monkey Wrench
8" block
Make 13.

Cutting

All measurements include ¼"-wide seam allowances.

From each 5" x 10" yellow or cream rectangle, cut:

2 squares, each 4⅜". Cut the squares once diagonally to make 4 half-square triangles, for a total of 52 triangles.

From each 5" x 10" violet rectangle, cut:

2 squares, each 4⅜". Cut the squares once diagonally to make 4 half-square triangles, for a total of 52 triangles.

From the yellow or cream print scraps, cut:

52 rectangles, each 1½" x 3"

From the green and blue-green print scraps, cut:

52 squares, each 1½"

Enough 1"-wide strips to make 2 strips, each 1" x 42"

From the violet print scraps, cut:

13 squares, each 1½"

From the multi-colored violet print, cut:

2 squares, each 13¾". Cut the squares twice diagonally to make 8 side setting triangles.

2 squares, each 7¾". Cut the squares once diagonally to make 4 corner setting triangles.

From the black (dark value) print, cut:

1 strip, 3½" x 42", for top inner border*

2 strips, each 2" x 42", for side inner borders

1 strip, 4½" x 42", for bottom inner border*

Cut strips from the lengthwise grain if stripes run the length of the fabric.

From the multi-colored (dark value) print, cut:

1 strip, 6½" x 42", for top outer border

3 strips, each 5½" x 42", for side outer borders

1 strip, 9½" x 42", for bottom outer border

To make 1 block:

1. Join a yellow and a violet triangle. Make 4 matching units.

Make 4.

2. Join a yellow rectangle and a green or blue-green square. Make 4 units.

Make 4.

3. Join the units, placing a violet square in the center, to make 1 Monkey Wrench block. Make 13 blocks.

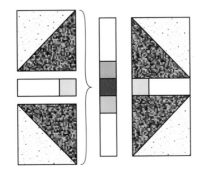

Make 13.

Quilt Top Assembly and Finishing

1. Arrange the blocks and side setting triangles in diagonal rows. The triangles are cut larger than necessary to allow for trimming in step 2. Join to form rows. Join the rows, adding the corner setting triangles last.

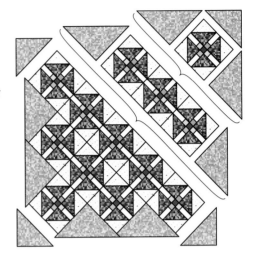

2. Trim the quilt top, leaving ½" of fabric beyond the block points.

3. Add the top and bottom inner borders.

4. Piece the 1"-wide green and blue-green strips end to end to make 2 strips, each 42" long. Join them to the side inner borders. Add the side inner borders.

5. Add the top and bottom outer borders. Add the side outer borders.

6. Layer the quilt top with batting and backing; baste. Quilt as desired.

7. *Optional:* embroider the block seams in feather stitches.

8. Bind the edges with pieced strips of violet prints.

9. *Optional:* embellish the quilt with beads.

Pink Tulips

by Laura Munson Reinstatler

Pink Tulips *by Laura Munson Reinstatler, 1996, Mill Creek, Washington, 24" x 24¼". Low-intensity versions of complementary red and green set a serene, sophisticated mood in this contemporary composition.*

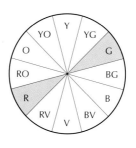

Finished Size: 24" x 24¼"
Skill Level: Intermediate

Color Cues

Laura finds working with complements a challenge. For her, the most comfortable method is to work with 80% to 90% of one color, and 10% to 20% of its complement.

While it's easy to create high contrast using complements, a quiet effect can be difficult. To calm an energetic palette, or to achieve an even balance of hues, Laura uses lower-intensity colors or cheats a little by pushing the hues toward their neighbors. For "Pink Tulips," the pinks range from pale melons (red-orange) through true reds to hints of magenta (red-violet). The greens include touches of blue with a few yellows and even some oranges. Subtle color shifts allow the hues to work together smoothly, creating rich harmony and depth.

The realistic design of "Pink Tulips" offers the freedom to place the vase, tulips, and leaves in a natural arrangement. Subtle discrepancies from the pattern will not sacrifice the pleasing appearance of the appliqué. Experiment with the vase, leaf, and tulip placement to make the design more personal.

Materials: 44"-wide fabric

½ yd. green lengthwise stripe for background and binding
⅛ yd. multi-colored stripe for background
1 rectangle, 10¼" x 21¼", of green leaf print for background
1 rectangle, 14½" x 16", of white-on-cream print for background
1 square, 10½", of gray print for vase
Assorted green print scraps for leaves and stems
Assorted pink scraps for tulips
26" square for backing
26" square of batting

Cutting

When cutting, orient stripes as shown.

From the green stripe, cut:
1 rectangle, 4¾" x 14½", for background
1 strip, 1⅞" x 24¼", for background
Reserve the remaining fabric for binding.

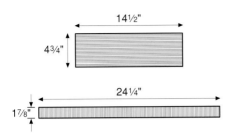

From the multi-colored stripe, cut:
1 strip, 1½" x 14½", for background
1 strip, 1⅞" x 24¼", for background

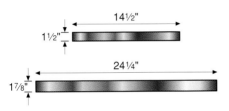

Assembly

1. Join the background rectangles and strips as shown.

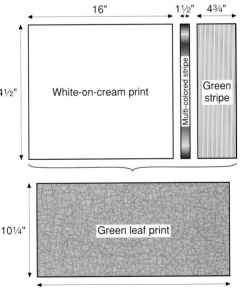

2. Prepare the appliqué pieces using your favorite method and the templates on pages 105–106. Cut pieces 12 and 13 from the same fabric; both are parts of the same leaf.

3. Position the vase on the background and pin in place; then baste to make placing pieces 1–7 easier.

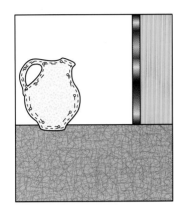

4. Appliqué leaves and stems 1–7 in numerical order; then appliqué the vase.

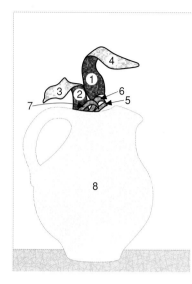

5. Appliqué leaves 9–11.

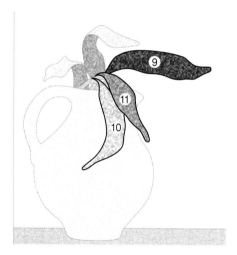

6. Appliqué leaves and stems 12–17.

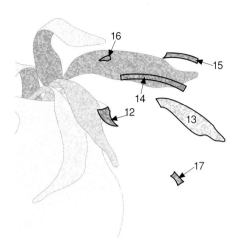

7. Appliqué tulips 18–53 in numerical order.

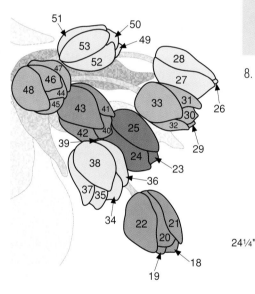

Tip: Laura found it easiest to join each tulip's petals to make one blossom, and then appliqué the tulip to the background as one piece.

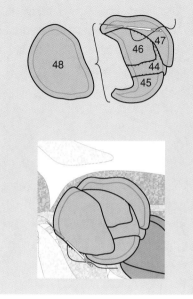

8. Add the 1⅞" x 24¼" green stripe and the 1⅞" x 24¼" multi-color print strips to the quilt top.

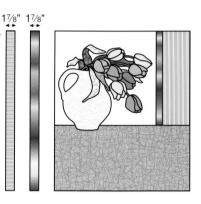

9. Layer the quilt top with batting and backing; baste.
10. Quilt as desired. Laura quilted along the lines in the printed fabrics.
11. Bind the edges.

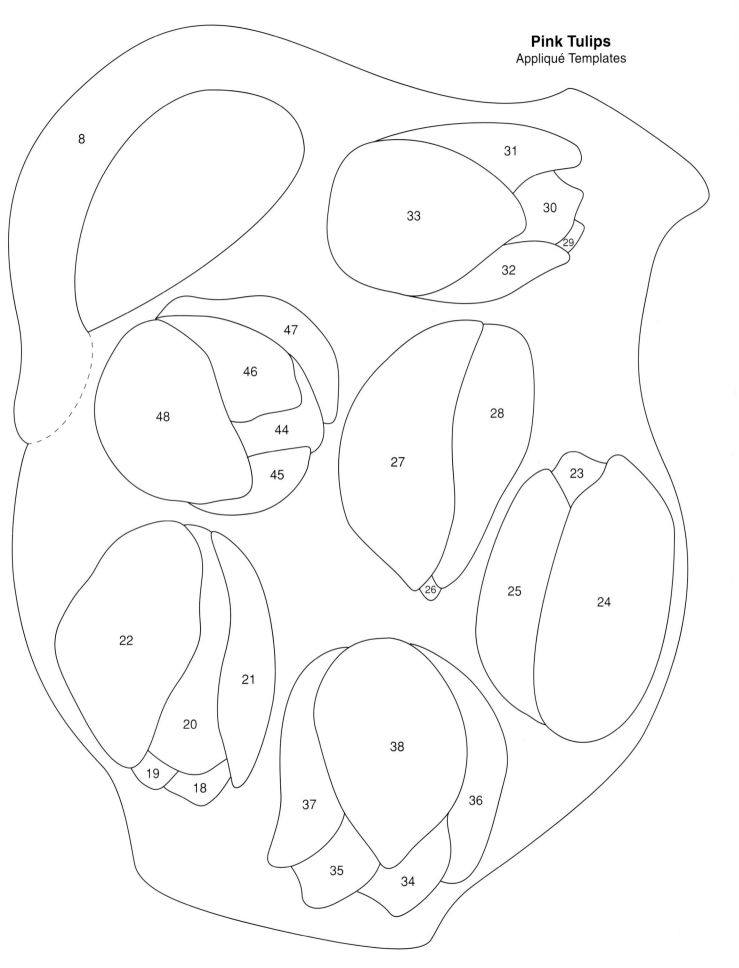

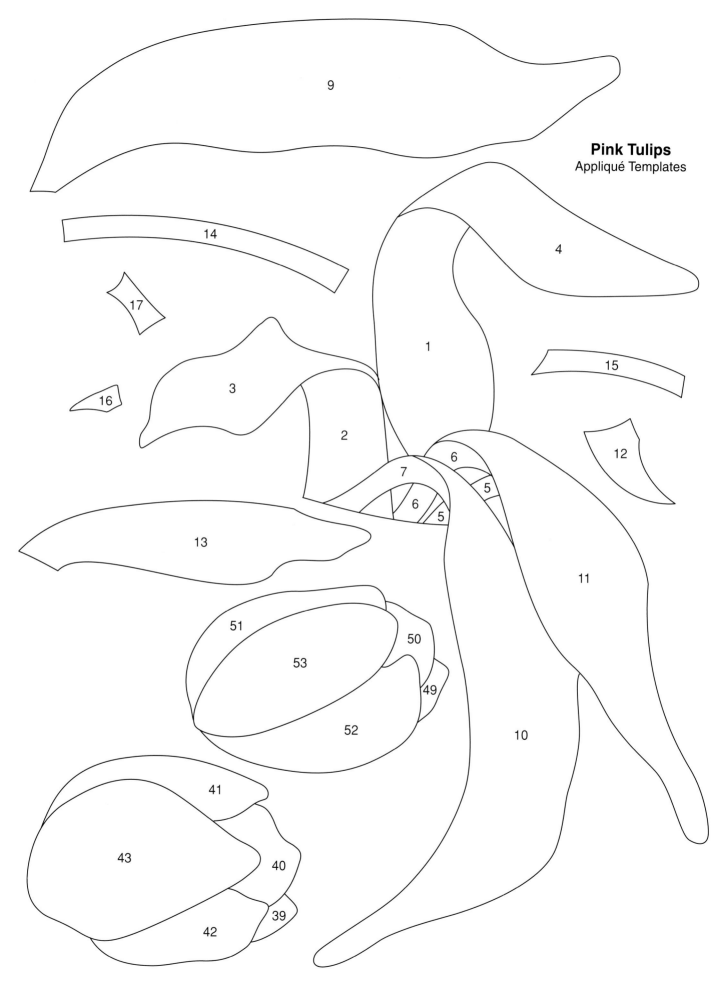

Pink Tulips
Appliqué Templates

Free As a Bird

by Wendy Hill

Free As a Bird *by Wendy Hill, 1996, Sunriver, Oregon, 72½" x 72½".*
Complementary colors mix it up in this free-wheeling interpretation of Wild
Goose Chase. Variations in value help to create a quilt that is alive with
sparkling color and dappled light.

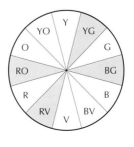

Finished Size: 72½" x 72½"
Skill Level: Beginner

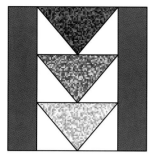

Wild Goose Chase
6" block
Make 144.

Color Cues

This spirited variation of Wild Goose Chase relies on a simple repeat block and strict color and value placement for its graphic impact. The color combination is a true double split complement (page 18): complementary red and green have been split into red-violet and red-orange, and yellow-green and blue-green. The red-violet and yellow-green are complements; so are the red-orange and blue-green.

Within this classic combination, Wendy has stretched the color families to include many versions of each hue in a variety of values and intensities. Neutrals that range from white to beige flutter randomly across the surface.

The visual sophistication of "Free As a Bird" belies its simple construction. Foundation piecing on a muslin base makes it easy to assemble the blocks quickly and accurately.

To help you collect a variety of harmonious fabrics, make a color chart for each of the four color families. Start each chart with a piece of fabric that is a genuine version of the color—a true red-violet, for example. Glue a 1" swatch of the fabric to the center of a sheet of paper. As you shop, refer to your chart and add swatches of your new fabrics; soon you will have a blooming record of your color scheme.

Materials: 44"-wide fabric

5 yds. lightweight muslin for foundation squares

1 yd. total of assorted light values in each of the 4 color families (red-violet, yellow-green, red-orange, and blue-green) for geese and rectangles*

1 yd. total of assorted medium values in each of the 4 color families (red-violet, yellow-green, red-orange, and blue-green) for geese and rectangles*

1 yd. total of assorted dark values in each of the 4 color families (red-violet, yellow-green, red-orange, and blue-green) for geese and rectangles*

5½ yds. total of assorted neutrals for background**

4½ yds. fabric for backing

¾ yd. fabric for binding

Batting

Graph paper

Sulky® iron-on transfer pen

*For the most economical use of fabric, buy in 6" increments (⅙ yd., ⅓ yd., ½ yd., etc.).

**For the most economical use of fabric, buy in 4½" increments (⅛ yd., ¼ yd., ⅜ yd., etc.).

Cutting

All measurements include generous seam allowances for foundation piecing.

From the muslin, cut:

24 strips, each 7" x 42". Crosscut strips into a total of 144 squares, each 7".

From the assorted light values in each color family (red-violet, yellow-green, red-orange, and blue-green), cut:

18 squares, each 5".* Cut each square once diagonally to make 2 half-square triangles for a total of 36 triangles in each color family.

12 rectangles, each 5" x 7½". Cut each rectangle in half lengthwise to make 2 rectangles, each 2½" x 7½", for a total of 24 rectangles in each color family.

From the assorted medium values in each color family (red-violet, yellow-green, red-orange, and blue-green), cut:

18 squares, each 5".* Cut each square once diagonally to make 2 half-square triangles for a total of 36 triangles in each color family.

12 rectangles, each 5" x 7½". Cut each rectangle in half lengthwise to make 2 rectangles, each 2½" x 7½", for a total of 24 rectangles in each color family.

From the assorted dark values in each color family (red-violet, yellow-green, red-orange, and blue-green), cut:

18 squares, each 5".* Cut each square once diagonally to make 2 half-square triangles for a total of 36 triangles in each color family.

12 rectangles, each 5" x 7½". Cut each rectangle in half lengthwise to make 2 rectangles, each 2½" x 7½", for a total of 24 rectangles in each color family.

From the neutrals, cut:

3 squares, each 4", from the same fabric. Cut the squares once diagonally to make a set of 6 triangles. Cut a total of 144 sets of 6 matching triangles.

*For directional fabric, make a template from the large triangle on your master block (see below), adding a generous ⅝"-wide seam allowance.

Transferring the Block Design

1. On graph paper, draft the block using the dimensions given below. Using a grid ruler, mark each line on your master block with the iron-on transfer pen.

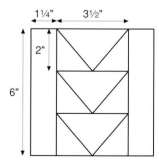

2. Center the master block, ink side down, over a muslin square, leaving an even margin on all sides. Follow the manufacturer's instructions to transfer the design to the muslin.

Piecing the Blocks

Each block contains 2 complementary colors and 1 neutral. The geese triangles in each block are light, medium, and dark values of one color family (red-violet, for example); the rectangles are a light, medium, or dark version of the complementary color (yellow-green, for example). Refer to the illustrations below for the color and value placement.

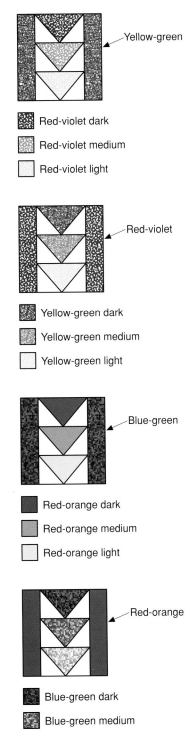

Yellow-green

Red-violet dark

Red-violet medium

Red-violet light

Yellow-green dark

Yellow-green medium

Yellow-green light

Red-violet

Blue-green

Red-orange dark

Red-orange medium

Red-orange light

Red-orange

Blue-green dark

Blue-green medium

Blue-green light

You will position the pieces on the unlined side of the muslin foundation square and sew on the lined side. Sew the pieces to the muslin square in numerical order as shown below.

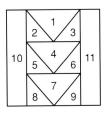

Piecing order

1. With the unlined side of a muslin square facing up, center a colored triangle (piece 1) right side up so that the edges extend beyond the seam lines marked on the lined side. (The shape of piece 1 is slightly different from the triangle marked on the muslin.) Pin piece 1 in place on the unlined side.

Unlined side of muslin

2. With right sides together, position a neutral triangle (piece 2) on piece 1 over the shared seam line. (Note that the cut edges of pieces 1 and 2 are not aligned.) Place a temporary pin along the seam line; flip piece 2 right side up and check the placement. The edges of piece 2 should extend beyond the marked seam lines and be approximately on-grain; remove the pin and reposition the piece, if necessary. When correctly positioned, pin piece 2 beyond the seam line.

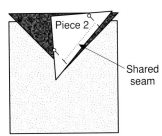

Tip: To help you position each successive piece, place a pin at each end of the marked seam to be sewn on the lined side of the muslin square.

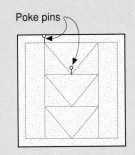

Poke pins

Lined side of muslin

Turn the square to the unlined side and visualize the seam line between the two pins. Position the triangle; then remove the pins.

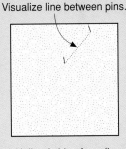

Visualize line between pins.

Unlined side of muslin

3. Turn the muslin square to the lined side and sew on the shared seam line, starting and stopping the seam ⅛" beyond each end.

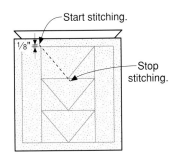

Start stitching.

⅛"

Stop stitching.

Lined side of muslin

Turn the square over and flip piece 2 right side up; check the placement again. Trim the seam allowance and press piece 2 in place.

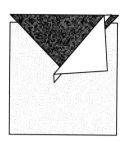

4. Add piece 3 in the same manner as piece 2.

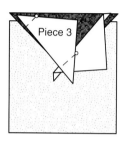

Piece 3

Add the remaining pieces in numerical order.

> *Tip:* It saves time to mass-produce the blocks in groups of twelve rather than making one at a time.

5. Square up and trim the blocks from the lined side, leaving a ⅜"-wide seam allowance. Zigzag the edges.

> *Note:* Wendy uses a ⅜"-wide seam allowance to join the blocks because the layer of muslin adds weight to the quilt. She zigzags the edges to keep the layers together and stabilize the blocks before assembling the quilt top.

Assembling the Quilt Top

1. Sort the blocks into the 4 color families, identifying the blocks by the color of the geese; that is, blocks with red-orange geese, blocks with blue-green geese, and so on.

2. Referring to the photo on page 107 and the illustration below, arrange the blocks on your design wall in groups of 4, one block from each color family. Strive to evenly distribute the light, medium, and dark rectangles across the quilt. Separate blocks that have the same neutral fabrics.

Blue-green   Red-violet

Yellow-green   Red-orange

3. Sew 4 blocks together to make 1 unit, using a ⅜"-wide seam allowance. Press the seams open.

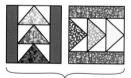

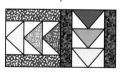

Maintaining the same color orientation, repeat with the remaining blocks until all are sewn into units of 4.

4. Sew 2 units together to make a section. Repeat with the remaining units.

Unit   Section

5. Sew 3 sections together to make a row. Make a total of 6 rows.

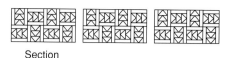

Section

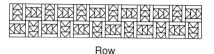

Row

6. Sew rows 1, 2, and 3 together to make half of the quilt top. Repeat with rows 4, 5, and 6.

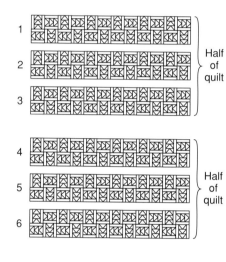

7. Sew the halves together to complete the quilt top.

Finishing

1. Layer the quilt top with batting and backing; baste.

2. Machine quilt in-the-ditch between the blocks or choose a free-form design. (Hand quilting is not recommended because of the thickness of the quilt sandwich.)

3. Bind the edges.

Stars Out of Africa

by Susan Gilliam Dileanis

Stars Out of Africa *by Susan Gilliam Dileanis, 1995, Sacramento, California, 59" x 71". Inspired by the rectangular designs in African weavings, Susan created an elongated version of the classic Variable Star block. A mélange of African and commercial quilting fabrics in a variety of values and smoldering hues carries out the ethnic mood.*

Finished Size: 59" x 71"
Skill Level: Advanced

Star
9" x 11" block
Make 25.

Color Cues

Subtle contrasts and complex color harmonies set a mood of quiet sophistication in this original star quilt. Susan began with a group of African fabrics, which were a gift, then added a variety of quilting fabrics for a total of eighty-five pieces. Her biggest challenge was finding transition fabrics to bridge the color gaps between the African prints.

The stars are composed of assorted medium and dark values, surrounded by light-value background fabrics. (Squint, and you'll see oval halos around every other star, the result of alternating medium-light and light background pieces.) A pieced border frames the stars and accentuates their elongated lines.

This quilt features a triad of low-intensity, secondary green, violet, and orange, extended to include red, but you can use any color combination as long as your cast of fabrics includes a wide range of values. No matter what scheme you choose, work out the quilt plan on your design wall, before your sew, to make sure that each star contains matching pieces and the corner triangles coordinate from block to block.

Materials: 44"-wide fabric

1¾ yds. *total* assorted dark-value fabrics for blocks and pieced border

2 yds. *total* assorted medium-value fabrics for blocks

1 yd. *total* assorted medium-light–value fabrics for blocks

1⅛ yds. *total* assorted light-value fabrics for blocks

1¾ yds. medium-light–value fabric for border

3½ yds. fabric for backing (crosswise seam)

½ yd. dark-value fabric for binding

Batting

Cutting

Use the templates on pages 116–17.

From the dark-value fabrics, cut:

4 template A and 4 template A reversed from the same fabric for the star points. Cut a total of 25 sets of 8 same-fabric triangles.

30 template A and 30 template A reversed for the border

25 template D; 1 for center of each block

From the medium-value fabrics, cut:

2 template A and 2 template A reversed from the same fabric to surround each piece D. Cut a total of 25 sets of 4 same-fabric triangles.

2 template A and 2 template A reversed from the same fabric for the corners of each block. Cut a total of 25 sets of 4 same-fabric triangles.

30 template A and 30 template A reversed for the border

116 template E, 4 from the same fabric for each block; plus 16 for the border

From the medium-light–value fabrics, cut:

Note: For each block you will need 2 piece A and 2 piece A reversed, 4 piece B, and 4 piece C, all cut from the same fabric.

2 template A and 2 template A reversed for the corners of each block. Cut a total of 12 sets of 4 same-fabric triangles.

60 template B, 4 from the same fabric for each block and 12 for the border

60 template C, 4 from the same fabric for each block and 12 for the border

From the light-value fabrics, cut:

Note: For each block you will need 2 piece A and 2 piece A reversed, 4 piece B, and 4 piece C, all cut from the same fabric.

2 Template A and 2 template A reversed for the corners of each block. Cut a total of 13 sets of 4 same-fabric triangles.

60 template B, 4 from the same fabric for each block and 8 for the border

60 template C, 4 from the same fabric for each block and 8 for the border

From the medium-light–value border fabric, cut:

2 lengthwise strips, each 2¾" x 45½", for top and bottom borders

2 lengthwise strips, each 2¾" x 55½", for side borders

8 template F, for top and bottom borders

8 template G, for side borders

2 rectangles, each 13¾" x 17⅜". Cut the rectangles once diagonally as shown to make 2 piece H and 2 piece H reversed for the corners of the quilt.

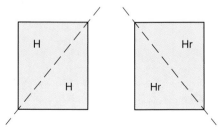

To make 1 block:

Note: The sample block has medium-light background pieces.

1. Using template 1A, trim the corners of the medium and medium-light triangles for easier piecing. For the block corners, sew 1 medium-light A to 1 medium A to make Unit 1. Sew 1 medium-light A reversed to 1 medium A reversed to make Unit 1 reversed. Press the seam toward the medium fabric.

Unit 1
Make 2.

Unit 1 reversed
Make 2.

2. For the upper and lower sections of the block, sew 1 medium-light B to 1 medium E. (Note the position of the 80° angle in E.) Press the seam toward B. Repeat with another medium-light B. Make 2 units.

Make 2.

3. Using template 2A, trim the corners of 2 dark triangles. Sew 1 dark A to one of the units made in the preceding step. Press the seam toward A. Repeat with a dark A reversed to make Unit 2. Make 2 units.

Unit 2
Make 2.

4. For the sides of the block, sew 1 medium-light C to 1 medium E. (Note the position of the 80° angle in E.) Press the seam toward C. Repeat with another medium-light C. Make 2 units.

Make 2.

5. Using template 3A, trim the corners of 2 dark triangles. Sew 1 dark A reversed to one of the units made in the preceding step. Press the seam toward A. Repeat with a dark A to make Unit 3. Make 2 units.

Unit 3
Make 2.

6. Using template 3A, trim the corners of 4 medium triangles. For the block center, sew 1 medium A to D. Press the seam toward A. Repeat with another medium A on the opposite edge. Add 2 medium A reversed pieces to make Unit 4.

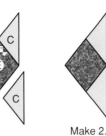

Unit 4
Make 1.

7. For the upper and lower sections of the block, sew a Unit 1 reversed to the left side of a Unit 2 as shown. Add a Unit 1

to the right side. Press the seams toward Unit 1. Make 2 units.

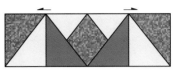

Make 2.

8. Sew a Unit 3 to each side of a Unit 4. Press the seams toward Unit 4.

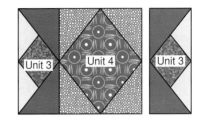

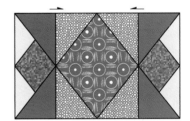

Make 1.

9. Sew the upper and lower sections to the center section to make 1 medium-light–background Star block. Press the seams away from Unit 4.

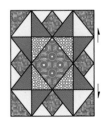

10. Make a total of 25 blocks, 12 with medium-light backgrounds and 13 with light backgrounds. Press the seams as

indicated above for the medium-light–background blocks; press the seams in the opposite directions on the light-background blocks in steps 7–9.

11. Arrange the blocks in 5 rows of 5 blocks each, alternating medium-light and light backgrounds. Join the blocks into rows. Join the rows.

Border Assembly

1. For the top and bottom borders, make 6 of Unit 2 with medium-light backgrounds and 4 of Unit 2 with light backgrounds. For the side borders, make 6 of Unit 3 with medium-light backgrounds, and 4 of Unit 3 with light backgrounds.

2. For the top and bottom borders, press under ¼" on 2 edges of E. (Note the position of the 80° angle in E.) Make a total of 8. For the side borders, press under ¼" on 2 edges of E. Make a total of 8.

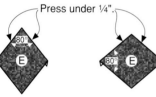

Make 8
for top and
bottom borders.

Make 8
for side borders.

3. For the top and bottom borders, appliqué the pressed edges of E to the apex of F, with the raw edges aligned and the pressed edges toward the center. Make a total of 8.

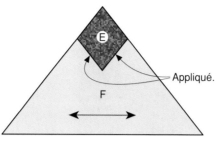

Make 8.

4. Sew a medium or dark (your choice) A and A reversed to each side of a Unit 2. Because the long edge of A is on the bias, gently press the seams away from Unit 2. Make 10 units, 6 with medium-light backgrounds and 4 with light backgrounds.

Make 6 medium-light background.
Make 4 light background.

5. Sew 1 A and 1 A reversed (medium or dark) together. Gently press the seam in either direction. Make 10 units. Sew this to the lower edge of the unit made in step 4 to make Unit 2A. Gently press the seam away from Unit 2.

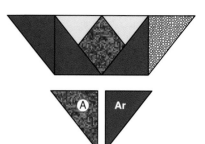

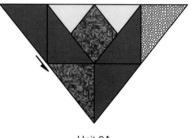

Unit 2A
Make 10.

6. Sew an appliquéd F triangle to a medium-light–background Unit 2A. Press the seam toward F.

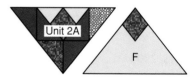

7. Continue joining 2A units and F triangles, alternating medium-light and light backgrounds so the medium-light–background units are at the ends and the middle of the border. Make another set.

Make 2.

8. Sew 1 medium-light border strip, 2¾" x 45½", to the edge of each border set made in the preceding step. Press the seams toward the border strips.

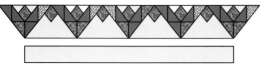

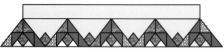

9. Sew the borders to the top and bottom edges of the quilt top. Press the seams toward the borders.

10. Make 2 side borders in the same manner as the top and bottom borders, using Unit 3, pieces A and A reversed, piece E, triangle G, and the medium-light border strips, each 2¾" x 55½". Alternate the medium-light and light backgrounds of Unit 3A so the medium-light–background units are at the ends and the middle of the border.

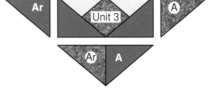

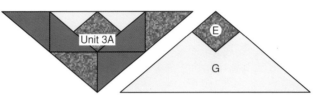

11. Sew the borders to the sides of the quilt top. Press the seams toward the borders.
12. Sew the medium-light H and H reversed triangles to the quilt corners as shown. Press the seams toward H and H reversed.

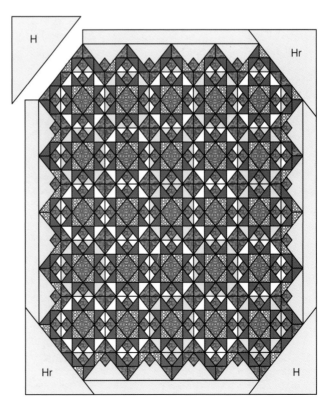

Finishing

1. Mark the quilt top for quilting as desired.
2. Layer the quilt top with batting and backing; baste.
3. Quilt as desired.
4. Bind the edges.

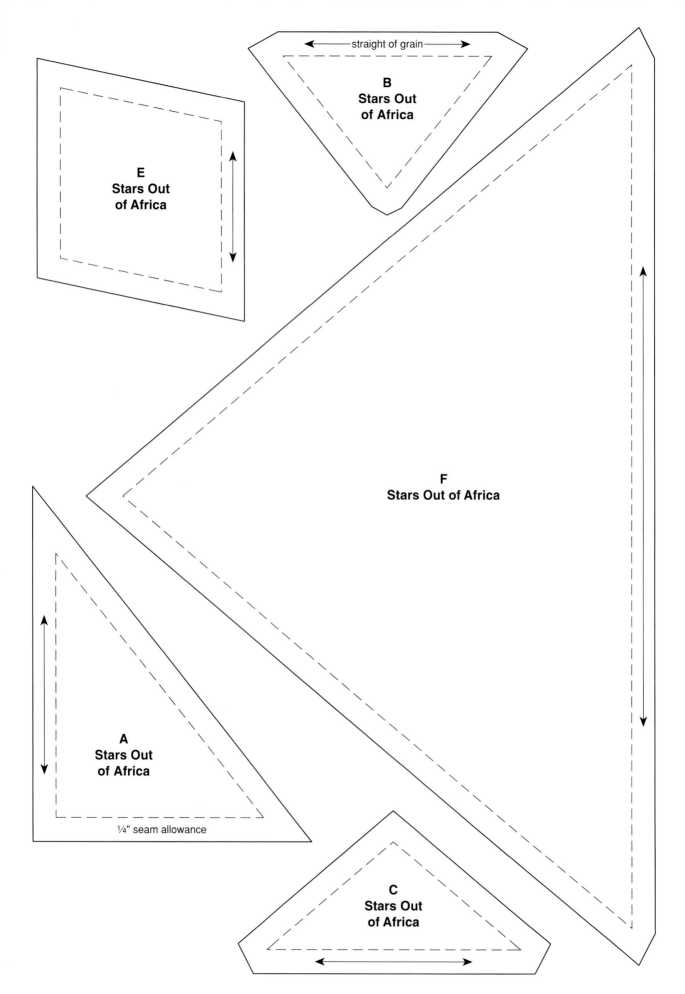

straight of grain

B
Stars Out
of Africa

E
Stars Out
of Africa

F
Stars Out of Africa

A
Stars Out
of Africa

¼" seam allowance

C
Stars Out
of Africa

straight of grain

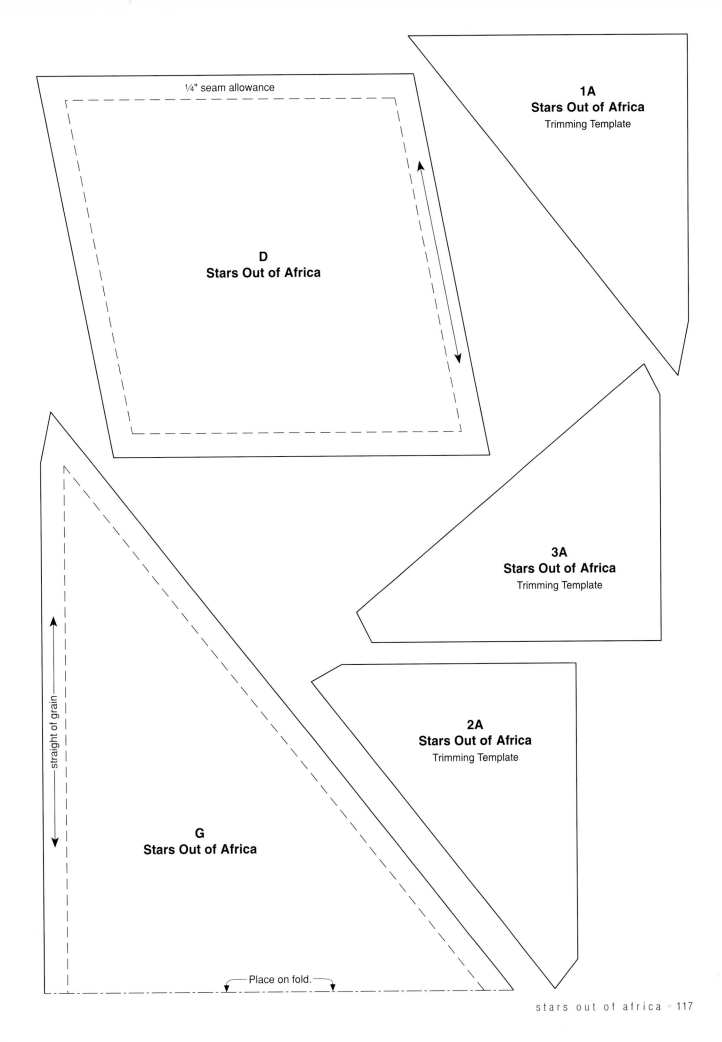

1A
Stars Out of Africa
Trimming Template

¼" seam allowance

D
Stars Out of Africa

3A
Stars Out of Africa
Trimming Template

2A
Stars Out of Africa
Trimming Template

straight of grain

G
Stars Out of Africa

Place on fold.

Tipsy Tiles
by Lynn Ticotsky

Tipsy Tiles *by Lynn M. Ticotsky, 1995, Cincinnati, Ohio, 50" x 64". Color and pattern dance across the surface of this vibrant quilt. Lynn began with a triad of secondary colors and a sophisticated tessellation, then played with the options, stretching, bending, and expanding the rules.*

Finished Size: 50" x 64"
Skill Level: Advanced

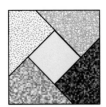

Single Block
7¼" block
Make 27.

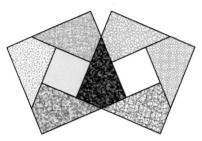

Interlocking Blocks

Note: This quilt is not for the faint of heart—or for brave beginners. It requires careful planning, lots of on-the-wall design time, and many inset and partial seams. Read all of the instructions carefully before you begin.

Color Cues

"Tipsy Tiles" came out of a tiling-pattern workshop Lynn took with Ruth McDowell. The class gave Lynn the chance to explore possibilities beyond the traditional block, to study the concept of tessellations, and to integrate quiltmaking and geometry. A photo of an Islamic tile floor made up of offset squares and interlocking trapezoids inspired her design.

Lynn is a great believer in intuitive quiltmaking, a process that encourages the quiltmaker to go beyond reproducing a pattern and into the realm of original art quilts. Lynn feels this approach makes the quilter a partner with her fabrics, permitting the maker and the materials to interact throughout the design process. Original design work also allows the quiltmaker to take full advantage of the clues arising from chance occurrences.

Lynn spends a great deal of time at her design board, composing the design and playing with the fabrics. Only by trying countless combinations of color, pattern, and texture—and standing back a good distance—can she see the full array of options. All of her decisions are made before construction begins.

The color scheme for "Tipsy Tiles," a triad (page 19) of orange, violet, and green, reaches far and wide to include many versions of each hue. A shot of "poison" in the form of yellow gives the quilt a heartbeat. Neutrals—actually, softer versions of oranges and yellows—provide breathing, calming spaces for the eye to rest

Two simple design concepts guided Lynn's color placement: First, the blocks that tilt to the right have orange centers, and those that tilt to the left have yellow centers. Second, the color is dark in the lower right corner of the quilt and fades to light in the upper left. Within those parameters, Lynn composed the quilt piece by piece on her design wall.

"Tipsy Tiles" is a true scrap quilt: Lynn used thirty-seven different fabrics, and all but two came from her stash. (She began with a lead fabric, which she eliminated as the design evolved.) It's essential to use a variety of patterns and textures—stripes, plaids, hand-dyed, polka dots, calicoes, near-solids, and representational prints. It's equally important to include a wide range of values (lights, mediums, and darks) and intensities (brights and dulls). For maximum design options, cut more trapezoids than you need and play with the possibilities. Make sure that a fabric appears at least twice in the quilt; the eye craves the repetition, and an orphan will stick out like a sore thumb.

Lynn chose a madras plaid for the setting triangles, cutting the pieces for the right and upper edges of the quilt from the warm areas of the plaid, and the pieces for the left and lower edges of the quilt from the cool areas. If you can't find a warm/cool plaid or print, choose a medium-value fabric that repeats colors used in the blocks.

The tilted border was pure happenstance. At the end of the workshop, Lynn and several friends quickly transferred her composition from the design wall to a large piece of muslin. In their haste, they pinned the pieces at an angle. Once home, Lynn liked the look and decided to draft wedge borders to frame the blocks.

Materials: 44"-wide fabric

½ yd. total assorted orange prints and solids for block center squares

½ yd. total assorted yellow prints and solids for block center squares

1⅛ yds. total assorted green prints and solids for blocks

1¼ yds. total assorted violet prints and solids for blocks

½ yd. total assorted neutral prints and solids for blocks

1 yd. medium-value plaid (or ⅝ yd. print) for setting triangles

⅝ yd. small-scale, dark violet print (Fabric 1) for wedge border

⅝ yd. large-scale, dark violet print (Fabric 2) for wedge border

⅝ yd. small-scale, medium-dark green print (Fabric 3) for wedge border

⅝ yd. large-scale, medium-dark green print (Fabric 4) for wedge border

3⅛ yds. fabric for backing (crosswise seam)

½ yd. assorted orange prints for binding

7 yds. ¼"-wide cotton twill tape

Protractor

Yardstick

Gridded pattern web for wedge border patterns

Batting

Cutting

Use the templates on pages 124–25.

Note: As you cut pieces using the templates, mark the seam-intersection dots.

From the assorted orange fabrics, cut:
27 Template A for block centers (Or rotary-cut 3½" squares.)

From the assorted yellow fabrics, cut:
27 Template A for block centers (Or rotary-cut 3½" squares.)

From the assorted green fabrics, cut:
49 Template B for blocks

From the assorted violet fabrics, cut:
58 Template B for blocks

From the assorted neutral fabrics, cut:
16 Template B for blocks

From the medium-value plaid or print, cut:
13 Template C
13 Template D
 2 Template E
 2 Template E reversed

Piecing the Blocks

Press the seams away from the center square as you add each piece.

Tip: It's easy to confuse the pieces once you begin to sew. To avoid frustration, make 27 photocopies of the basic block. Before you take down the pieces from your design board for the first block, note the position of each fabric on a diagram, including arrows for up and down. Piece the block according to the diagram, then return the block to its spot on the design board. Piece the remaining blocks in the same manner.

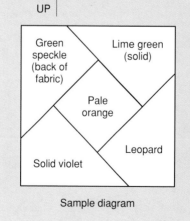

Sample diagram

1. Sew an orange square A and a trapezoid B together, starting at the corner and stopping at the point shown. Working in a clockwise direction, sew a second trapezoid to the unit just made. Add third and fourth trapezoids in the same manner. Finish the partial seam to complete the block. Make a total of 27 blocks.

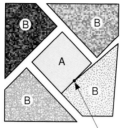

Partial seam

2. Sew a yellow square to the upper right edge of each block, starting at the right and stopping ¼" from the left edge at the seam-intersection dot; backstitch. Repeat for all blocks.

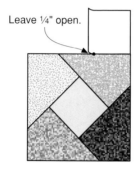

Leave ¼" open.

3. Sew the blocks together into offset rows, starting at the upper edge and stopping ¼" from the lower edge at the seam-intersection dot of the stepped-up block; backstitch. It's helpful to pin the seams where the trapezoids intersect.

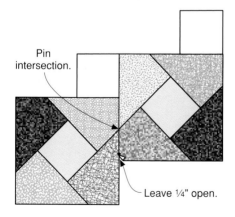

Pin intersection.

Leave ¼" open.

Joining the Rows

Note: On all seams that end at the perimeter of the pieced top, stop stitching ¼" from the edge, at the seam-intersection dots. This allows you to inset the setting triangles after the rows are joined.

Refer to the diagram below as you join the remaining squares and trapezoids to the rows, then join the rows:

1. Add 2 trapezoids to the upper right end of Row #1. Add a trapezoid to the upper right end of Row #2.
2. Join Rows #1 and #2. Start the seam at the dot, ¼" from the edge. Stop sewing

at the dot on the first yellow square; backstitch and clip the threads. Sew the remaining free side of the yellow square to Row #1, again stopping at the dot, backstitching, and clipping the threads. If you are experienced at inset piecing, you can leave the needle down at each 90° turn, pivot, then continue stitching.

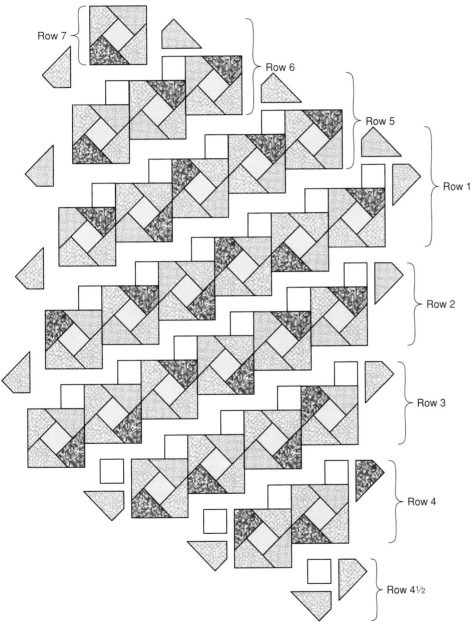

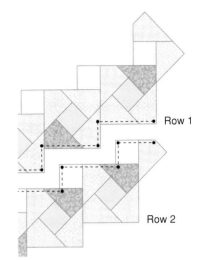

3. Add a trapezoid to the upper right end of Row #3. Repeat for Row #4. For the lower left end of Row #3, join a yellow square and a trapezoid; then sew this unit to the end of the row. Repeat for Row #4. Join the rows.

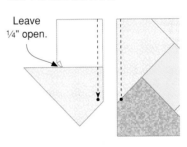

Leave ¼" open.

Rows 3 and 4

4. For Row #4½, join a yellow square and a trapezoid; sew this unit to another trapezoid. Join the row.

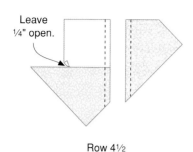

Row 4½

5. For Row #5, add a trapezoid to the upper edge. Repeat for Row #6. Join the rows.
6. Once all the rows are joined, inset the 4 remaining trapezoids on the left edge of the quilt top.

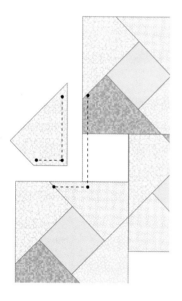

Adding the Setting Triangles

Inset the setting triangles just as you joined the rows, starting and stopping stitching at the seam-intersection dots.

1. Inset triangle C at the outer edge where 2 trapezoids meet and form a wide angle. Stitch from the edge to the apex of triangle C, starting and stopping stitching at the seam-intersection dots. Repeat with the remaining C triangles.
2. Inset the D triangles in the same way. Add the E and E reversed triangles to the corners.

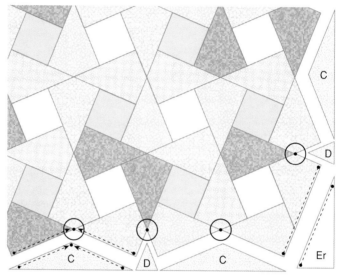

Lower right corner

Cutting, Piecing, and Attaching the Wedge Borders

Using gridded pattern web, a protractor, and a yardstick, enlarge the patterns for the wedge borders according to the measurements and angles below.

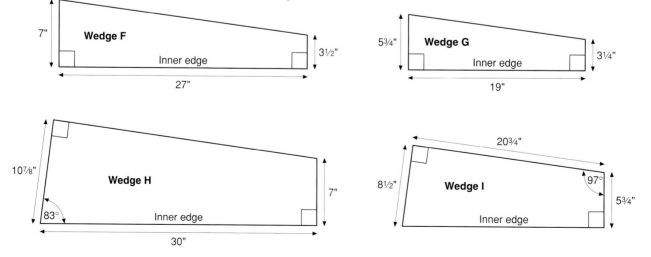

From the small-scale, dark violet print (Fabric #1), cut:

1 each of Wedges G and H

From the large-scale, dark violet print (Fabric #2), cut:

1 each of Wedges F and I

From the small-scale, medium-dark green print (Fabric #3), cut:

1 each of Wedges G and H

From the large-scale, medium-dark green print (Fabric #4), cut:

1 each of Wedges F and I

Piece and attach the wedge borders in a clockwise direction following the instructions and the illustration below.

1. Start with the bottom border. Sew G (Fabric #3) to I (Fabric #2). Sew this unit to the bottom edge of the quilt top with a partial seam; stop stitching 2" from the right corner.

2. For the left border, sew F (Fabric #4) to H (Fabric #3). Sew this unit to the left edge of the quilt top and bottom border.

3. For the top border, sew G (Fabric #1) to I (Fabric #4). Sew this unit to the top edge of the quilt top and left border.

4. For the right border, sew F (Fabric #2) to H (Fabric #1). Sew this unit to the top border and right edge of the quilt top. Complete the partial seam on the bottom border.

Finishing

1. Square up the edges and corners of the quilt top.

2. Mark the quilt top for quilting. The block pieces and setting triangles were quilted in-the-ditch, and the blocks were quilted in a pattern of concentric squares. Quilt the borders as desired.

3. Layer the quilt top with batting and backing; baste. Quilt.

4. In squaring up the corners and edges, you may have compromised the straight of grain. To prevent the quilt top from stretching, stitch ¼"-wide twill tape to the edges.

5. Bind the edges.

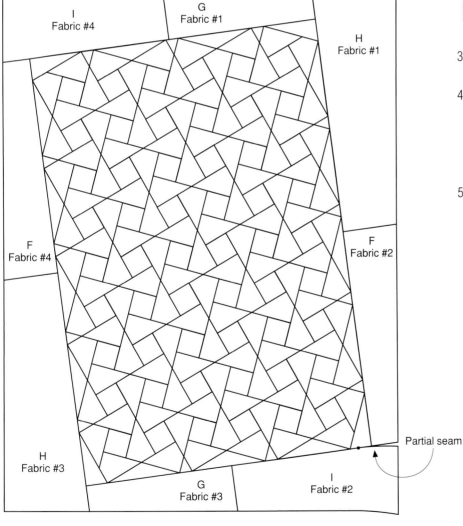

I
Fabric #4

G
Fabric #1

H
Fabric #1

F
Fabric #4

F
Fabric #2

H
Fabric #3

G
Fabric #3

I
Fabric #2

Partial seam

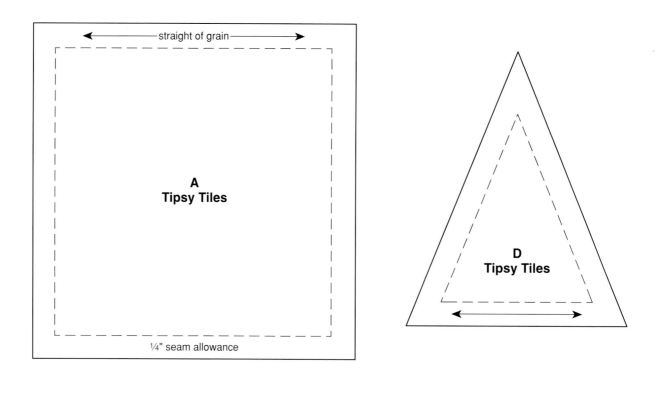

straight of grain

A
Tipsy Tiles

¼" seam allowance

D
Tipsy Tiles

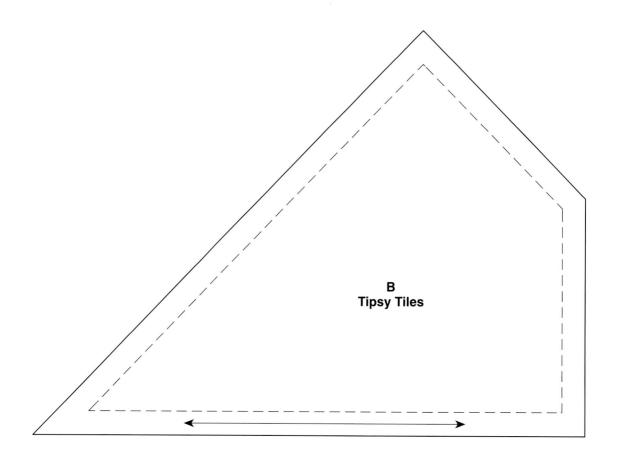

B
Tipsy Tiles

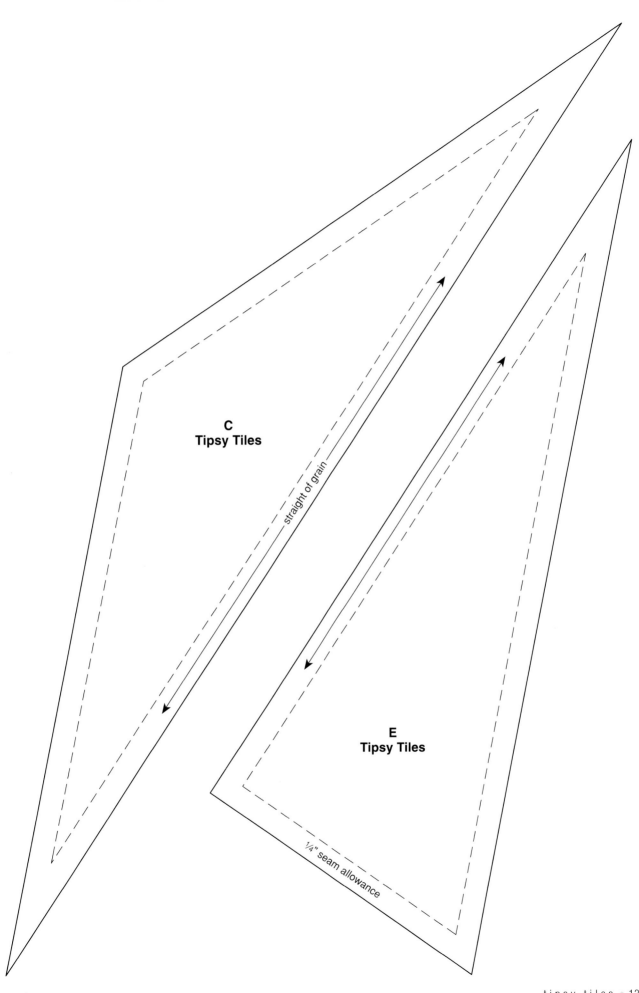

C
Tipsy Tiles

straight of grain

E
Tipsy Tiles

¼" seam allowance

About the Author

Christine Barnes is a freelance writer and editor of quiltmaking and home-decorating books who holds degrees in design and journalism. She has edited several titles for That Patchwork Place and, most recently, was "the pen behind the words" in the Fiber Studio Press title, *Velda Newman: A Painter's Approach to Quilt Design*. Christine prints fabric, stitches contemporary and Crazy quilts, and teaches classes in Crazy quilting and color for quilters. She lives in Grass Valley, a historic gold-mining town in northern California.

Bibliography

Albers, Josef. *Interaction of Color*. New Haven, Conn.: Yale University Press, 1963. A classic color text. Fascinating material, but dense, with few color photos.

Beyer, Jinny. *Jinny Beyer's Color Confidence for Quilters*. San Francisco: The Quilt Digest Press, 1992. A sophisticated approach to working with color using Beyer's color system and master palette.

Guild, Tricia. *Tricia Guild on Color*. New York: Rizzoli, 1993. A visual feast of color, pattern, and texture. Aimed at an audience interested in interior design, it is inspiring to anyone who works with color.

Itten, Johannes. *The Art of Color*. New York: Van Nostrand Reinhold, 1973. The classic work on color theory and a great source of information and inspiration to artists in all media.

Penders, Mary Coyne. *Color and Cloth: The Quiltmaker's Ultimate Workbook*. San Francisco: The Quilt Digest Press, 1989. An excellent resource for quilters. Exercises throughout.

Quiller, Stephen. *Color Choices: Making Color Sense Out of Color Theory*. New York: Watson-Guptill Publications, 1989. Geared to painters, this book is helpful to quilters as well. Excellent examples of color combinations.

Sargent, Walter. *The Enjoyment and Use of Color*. New York: Dover Publications, Inc., 1964. Another color classic, with in-depth, complex information. Challenging, but very few visuals.

Walch, Margaret, and Augustine Hope. *Living Colors: The Definitive Guide to Color Palettes Through the Ages*. San Francisco: Chronicle Books, 1995. Eighty color combinations, with detailed narrative, taken from art and history. An inspirational book for quilters.

Wolfrom, Joen. *The Magical Effects of Color*. Martinez, Calif.: C & T Publishing, 1992. In-depth coverage of the art and science of color, with additional design information. Extensive gallery.

Zelanski, Paul, and Mary Pat Fisher. *Color*. Englewood Cliffs, N.J.: Prentice Hall, 1994. For artists in all media. Thorough chapters on color systems and color combinations.

Index

Publications and Products

THAT PATCHWORK PLACE TITLES:

That Patchwork Place®
AMERICA'S BEST-LOVED QUILT BOOKS®

All the Blocks Are Geese • Mary Sue Suit
All New Copy Art for Quilters
All-Star Sampler • Roxanne Carter
Appliqué in Bloom • Gabrielle Swain
Appliquilt® • Tonee White
Appliquilt® for Christmas • Tonee White
Appliquilt® to Go • Tonee White
Appliquilt® Your ABCs • Tonee White
Around the Block with Judy Hopkins
At Home with Quilts • Nancy J. Martin
Baltimore Bouquets • Mimi Dietrich
Bargello Quilts • Marge Edie
Beyond Charm Quilts
　　• Catherine L. McIntee & Tammy L. Porath
Bias Square® Miniatures • Christine Carlson
Blockbender Quilts • Margaret J. Miller
Block by Block • Beth Donaldson
Borders by Design • Paulette Peters
Calicoes & Quilts Unlimited
　　• Judy Betts Morrison
The Cat's Meow • Janet Kime
Celebrate! with Little Quilts • Alice Berg,
　　Sylvia Johnson & Mary Ellen Von Holt
Celebrating the Quilt
Class-Act Quilts
*Classic Quilts with Precise Foundation
　　Piecing* • Tricia Lund & Judy Pollard
Color: The Quilter's Guide • Christine Barnes
Colourwash Quilts • Deirdre Amsden
Country Medallion Sampler • Carol Doak
Crazy Rags • Deborah Brunner
Decorate with Quilts & Collections
　　• Nancy J. Martin
Down the Rotary Road with Judy Hopkins
Dress Daze • Judy Murrah
The Easy Art of Appliqué
　　• Mimi Dietrich & Roxi Eppler
Easy Machine Paper Piecing • Carol Doak
*Easy Mix & Match Machine Paper
　　Piecing* • Carol Doak
Easy Paper-Pieced Keepsake Quilts
　　• Carol Doak
Easy Reversible Vests • Carol Doak
A Fine Finish • Cody Mazuran
*Five- and Seven-Patch Blocks & Quilts for
　　the ScrapSaver* • Judy Hopkins
*Four-Patch Blocks & Quilts for the
　　ScrapSaver* • Judy Hopkins
Freedom in Design • Mia Rozmyn
From a Quilter's Garden • Gabrielle Swain
Go Wild with Quilts • Margaret Rolfe
Go Wild with Quilts—Again! • Margaret Rolfe
Great Expectations • Karey Bresenhan
　　with Alice Kish & Gay E. McFarland

Hand-Dyed Fabric Made Easy
　　• Adriene Buffington
Happy Endings • Mimi Dietrich
Honoring the Seasons • Takako Onoyama
Jacket Jazz • Judy Murrah
Jacket Jazz Encore • Judy Murrah
The Joy of Quilting
　　• Joan Hanson & Mary Hickey
Kids Can Quilt • Barbara J. Eikmeier
Life in the Country with Country Threads
　　• Mary Tendall & Connie Tesene
Little Quilts • Alice Berg, Sylvia Johnson &
　　Mary Ellen Von Holt
Lively Little Logs • Donna McConnell
The Log Cabin Design Workbook
　　• Christal Carter
Loving Stitches • Jeana Kimball
*Machine Needlelace and Other
　　Embellishment Techniques* • Judy Simmons
Machine Quilting Made Easy • Maurine Noble
*Magic Base Blocks for Unlimited Quilt
　　Designs* • Patty Barney & Cooky Schock
Miniature Baltimore Album Quilts
　　• Jenifer Buechel
Mirror Manipulations • Gail Valentine
More Jazz from Judy Murrah
More Strip-Pieced Watercolor Magic
　　• Deanna Spingola
*Nine-Patch Blocks & Quilts for the
　　ScrapSaver* • Judy Hopkins
No Big Deal • Deborah L. White
Once upon a Quilt
　　• Bonnie Kaster & Virginia Athey
Patchwork Pantry
　　• Suzette Halferty & Carol C. Porter
A Perfect Match • Donna Lynn Thomas
A Pioneer Doll and Her Quilts • Mary Hickey
Press for Success • Myrna Giesbrecht
Quilted for Christmas, Book II
Quilted for Christmas, Book III
Quilted Landscapes • Joan Blalock
Quilted Legends of the West
　　• Judy Zehner & Kim Mosher
Quilted Sea Tapestries • Ginny Eckley
Quilting Design Sourcebook • Dorothy Osler
Quilting Makes the Quilt • Lee Cleland
Quilting Up a Storm • Lydia Quigley
Quilts: An American Legacy • Mimi Dietrich
Quilts for Baby • Ursula Reikes
Quilts for Red-Letter Days • Janet Kime
Quilts Say It Best • Eileen Westfall
Refrigerator Art Quilts • Jennifer Paulson
Repiecing the Past • Sara Rhodes Dillow
Rotary Riot • Judy Hopkins & Nancy J. Martin
Rotary Roundup
　　• Judy Hopkins & Nancy J. Martin
Round Robin Quilts
　　• Pat Magaret & Donna Slusser
Sensational Settings • Joan Hanson

Sew a Work of Art Inside and Out
　　• Charlotte Bird
*Shortcuts: A Concise Guide to Rotary
　　Cutting* • Donna Lynn Thomas
Simply Scrappy Quilts • Nancy J. Martin
Small Talk • Donna Lynn Thomas
Square Dance • Martha Thompson
Start with Squares • Martha Thompson
Strip-Pieced Watercolor Magic
　　• Deanna Spingola
Stripples • Donna Lynn Thomas
Sunbonnet Sue All Through the Year
　　• Sue Linker
Template-Free® Quilts and Borders
　　• Trudie Hughes
Through the Window & Beyond
　　• Lynne Edwards
The Total Bedroom • Donna Babylon
Traditional Blocks Meet Appliqué
　　• Deborah J. Moffett-Hall
Transitions • Andrea Balosky
True Style • Peggy True
Victorian Elegance • Lezette Thomason
Watercolor Impressions
　　• Pat Magaret & Donna Slusser
Watercolor Quilts
　　• Pat Magaret & Donna Slusser
Weave It! Quilt It! Wear It!
　　• Mary Anne Caplinger
Whimsies & Whynots • Mary Lou Weidman
WOW! Wool-on-Wool Folk Art Quilts
　　• Janet Carija Brandt

4", 6", 8" & metric Bias Square® • BiRangle™
Ruby Beholder® • ScrapMaster • Rotary Rule™
Rotary Mate™ • Bias Stripper®
Shortcuts to America's Best-Loved Quilts (video)

FIBER STUDIO PRESS TITLES:

FIBER STUDIO PRESS

Complex Cloth • Jane Dunnewold
*Erika Carter: Personal
　　Imagery in Art Quilts* • Erika Carter
Inspiration Odyssey • Diana Swim Wessel
The Nature of Design • Joan Colvin
*Velda Newman: A Painter's Approach
　　to Quilt Design* • Velda Newman with
　　Christine Barnes

Many titles are available at your local quilt shop.
For more information, write for a free color catalog
to That Patchwork Place, Inc., PO Box 118, Bothell,
WA 98041-0118 USA.

☎ U.S. and Canada, call **1-800-426-3126** for the
name and location of the quilt shop nearest you.
Int'l: 1-206-483-3313　**Fax:** 1-206-486-7596
E-mail: info@patchwork.com
Web: www.patchwork.com　　　　5.97